Praise for *The Art of Badassery*

"Jennifer goes beyond showing women how to feel empowered. She shows them how to take action to protect their peace and their power. A must-read, especially if you want to enhance your ability to be your

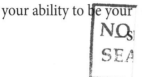

"Jennifer Cassetta is th... ...Badassery. This book is an empowering and inspiring step-by-step (or rather, belt-by-belt) guide to help you unleash your inner warrior and kick-start the black belt journey to your highest ambitions."

—**Kara Richardson Whitely,** author of *Gorge: My Journey Up Kilimanjaro at 300 Pounds* (soon to be a movie)

"There are books that talk about speaking up, unleashing your inner badass, and reclaiming your power, and then there are books that show you how to do it. *The Art of Badassery* shows you how to do it."

—**Jess Ekstrom,** author, *Chasing the Bright Side*

"As a mother, working hard to raise an empowered daughter, I was able to add some much-needed tools to my tool belt because of this book. It is not enough for us to tell our girls to be strong, but to empower them mentally, verbally, and physically without hesitation! A must-read as we fight for the next generation of girls to come."

—**Katie Wilcox,** founder and CEO of Natural Model Management

"For any woman who wants to find her inner badass, Jenn Cassetta knows the way! *The Art of Badassery* is a book we all need now—a time when it's more important than ever to own your mind, your body, and your future. Jenn provides a dynamic, funny, down-to-earth road map to becoming who you were born to be, giving step-by-step instructions on how to heal, how to grow, how to thrive."

         —Dana Belcastro, film producer and black belt

THE ART OF BADASSERY

UNLEASH YOUR MOJO WITH WISDOM OF THE DOJO

Jennifer Cassetta

Health Communications, Inc.
Boca Raton, Florida

www.hcibooks.com

Names and identifying characteristics of individuals
have been changed to protect their privacy.

Library of Congress Cataloging-in-Publication Data
is available through the Library of Congress

© 2022 Jennifer Cassetta

ISBN-13: 978-07573-2432-1 (Paperback)
ISBN-10: 07573-2432-0 (Paperback)
ISBN-13: 978-07573-2433-8 (ePub)
ISBN-10: 07573-2433-9 (ePub)

Publisher: Health Communications, Inc.
         1700 NW 2nd Avenue
         Boca Raton, FL 33432-1653

Cover design by Larissa Hise Henoch
Interior design and formatting by Larissa Hise Henoch

CONTENTS

INTRODUCTION

Do you feel like your confidence, your power, and your mojo have been drained, deflated, or you're just outright defeated? Have you been knocked down one too many times, and you're struggling to get back up with gusto? If so, my friend, you are in the perfect place. Even if you're feeling pretty badass already, you're still in the right place to level up. *The Art of Badassery* was created for you as a system to reclaim all of that precious power that may have been drained from you with every hit, loss, drama, trauma, or disappointment. I sourced this time-tested wisdom from martial arts and have used it in my keynotes and coaching programs with thousands of women who have gone from a life of blah to badassery. But first, let me tell you how I use this system in my own life.

In my early twenties, I was on my way to becoming an event planner until one day when my world turned upside down. It was a sunny Tuesday morning as I got onto the 6 Train toward downtown Manhattan to go to work. The event space where I worked had held its first event the night before, and I was excited to see my boss and hear how it went. As I neared Wall Street, the subway slowed and jerked a bit but finally let us off without a warning.

When I emerged from the subway, I looked up and saw the dark smoke billowing out of the World Trade Center. I was shocked and couldn't imagine what kind of accident could have done such damage. Everyone I passed on the street was pointing toward the ominous sight. When I walked three blocks to the corner of Rector and the West Side Highway, I saw a police officer staring up at the towers, sobbing. My heart sank. Even though I still had no idea what was happening, I knew it was bad.

I got to the building where I worked and spoke to the doorman. He told me I couldn't go upstairs because no one was there. "They bombed the towers," he said, "and the subways are shut down."

"Where should I go?" I shrieked. I was panicked and had no idea what to do. He shrugged and offered to let me use the phone in the lobby. Unsure who to call, I dialed my mom's work number, a call I can't remember making to this day.

My mom tells me I called her and in a childlike voice told her there was a hole in the World Trade Center. And that's when the first tower fell, sending a swarm of people rushing into the lobby seeking shelter. The phone went flying out of my hands, and I was pushed into a utility closet with a bunch of strangers. Poor Mom just heard people screaming because the phone didn't hang up for several minutes. To her it felt like hours.

While I'd love to tell you that I was the heroine of the story, comforting everyone and keeping them calm, I was not. I was paralyzed with fear and cried uncontrollably. A police officer told me to be quiet, and I remember thinking I was absolutely going to die in a closet with a bunch of strangers. Then a woman came over and put her hands on my shoulders. She asked me my name, and I told her. She said, "Jennifer, I'm Nancy, and you and I are going to get out of here today." I'm pretty sure I'd just met my guardian angel.

The officer made us all evacuate, concerned the building would collapse on top of us. Everyone scattered in different directions, and Nancy and I headed south. The ash was covering us like snowflakes, and we finally made it to 100 Broadway. There were people giving out masks and water, and for a few minutes we were okay. Shortly after the second tower fell, we had to evacuate 100 Broadway as well.

Nancy and I headed out again to find shelter. The martial arts school I had just started training at was nearby, and I figured we could go there to regroup. When we walked in, we must have looked like zombies, completely shell-shocked, and covered in dust. My instructors, Lena and Holly, were there, and for the first time that day I was able to exhale. I drank water, took a shower, and sat in front of a giant screen TV and heard for the first time what was actually happening in the world. Nancy took off soon after we arrived, and my efforts to try to find her since have been to no avail. (Nancy, if you're out there, thank you from the bottom of my heart.) I eventually made it uptown to my sister's apartment and then fled the city for a few days to unwind at my parents' house.

Once I returned to the city, I didn't feel safe. The clanging of garbage trucks sent me jumping out of my skin, the roar of an airplane engine overhead would make me want to take cover, and fireworks had me in full-out panic attack mode. And yet, all that fear disappeared in the martial arts school where I'd spend my days training. Wax on. Wax off. Follow the commands of the instructors. Kick, punch, sweat it all out, and end with some meditation. It was the best antianxiety medicine I could imagine. It was addictive but in the best way. That dojo became a source of safety and strength (aka, *dojang* in Korean, *dojo* in Japanese).

The more time I spent there, the better I felt. Physically, my body was getting stronger from all the conditioning. Mentally, I started to feel more confident as I learned life-saving skills. Spiritually, I started to feel more grounded and purposeful, more than I ever had in my life.

In the aftermath of the attack, I was out of a job like so many others at that time. That only added further inspiration to find a new path. Training in martial arts was helping me put myself back together, piece by piece. One day it occurred to me that it could be more than a hobby; it could become a new way of life.

It was during the next year that I decided that, somehow, I wanted to create a career that helped others feel strong, safe, and confident, just like I was beginning to feel. That was the beginning of my journey to becoming a motivational speaker, a self-defense and empowerment coach, and, most importantly, a black belt in badassery.

What Is the Art of Badassery?

A badass knows how to speak her truth, set boundaries, and block the bullshit that comes her way. She knows how to believe in herself and get back up after she's been knocked down. She knows how to fight for what's right, for what she deserves, and for causes bigger than herself.

We all have a badass inside just waiting to be unleashed. I

believe this because I've lived it myself, and I've seen it time and time again—in the women I coach and speak with at colleges, corporations, and conferences around the country.

I receive e-mails from college women who tell me stories of men breaking into their dorms or slipping blackout drugs into their drinks, and they want me to come speak at their campus. After I speak at organizations, women approach me and share their stories of being stalked or assaulted. I speak to women in the hospitality industry who are objectified, inappropriately touched, or spoken down to. I have professional women share their stories of how they are still being mansplained, overlooked for promotions, or have had their ideas stolen or repackaged by others. I hear from mothers who worry for the safety of their daughters who are heading out into the world on their own. This is the backdrop of what women face collectively.

We deserve better. But I think it has become abundantly clear that nobody is going to grant us what we deserve. We need to know how to stand up and fight for it—for ourselves and for one another. We need to learn how to walk through this world with confidence and strength. How to speak up in a powerful way so people listen. How to preserve our vital energy so we don't burn out or spend it all on people who are unworthy. How to trust our inner guidance and use all these lessons to make a better world. How to unleash our inner badass. These are the principles that I have been speaking about during my keynotes for the past decade that have inspired the pages of this book.

Unleashing your badassery requires the holistic mind-body-spirit strength of a warrior. Women under pressure have been demonstrating this warrior strength for centuries in order to make a bigger impact on the world. You are a warrior, as I'm sure you have taken a proverbial beating and had to stand up for yourself, your family, and/or a cause greater than yourself. This book will lead you to remember and reclaim that inner strength in your heart forever.

I see it over and over again in my work: Women are looking for an opportunity to develop their warrior skills because (1) the world needs our power and abilities, and (2) the world still, in the twenty-first century, is set up to deny us those opportunities. We must remember that we have been born into a patriarchal system that makes women forget how powerful we are and worthy of taking up space. We battle the patriarchy in small, insidious ways, like the pink tax (paying more for our razors and other self-care products), and we battle it in large, hideous ways, like women dying in massive numbers due to domestic abuse and sexual violence.

All the while men and boys get both explicit and implicit messages of their power and authority all the time. Did you grow up noticing that all the women in the kitchen prepared the food while the men watched football during holidays? Did your mom go to work and still shoulder most of the responsibility for taking care of the kids? Did Mom have access to her own money, or did she need to ask permission for it? Did you see women in leadership positions in your community, houses of worship, political representatives, or local businesses?

I have such clear memories of sitting in the church pews as a kid, listening to male priests, looking around for women in leadership positions, and never seeing them. I'd ask my parents why women weren't allowed to be priests, and I never received a satisfactory answer. I was lucky enough to grow up in a household where my parents encouraged me to follow my dreams. "You can be anything you want to be," they would say. Still, my sister and I had to clean the table while my brother sat and watched.

The messages we grew up with were confusing at best. We still feel the effects. Women now make up the majority of the workforce and yet still take on more of the household tasks than their partners. And still make less money than men. And still have not found equal political or social status. And are still touched without consent, harassed, and exploited. And still are not seen enough in positions of leadership and power.

The Path to Unleash Your Inner Badass

This book is a journey for your mind, body, and spirit, grass-hopper. In it, I use martial arts as an organizing principle and metaphor for several reasons:

1. It's what turned me and many women I know into badass warriors and women's empowerment advocates.
2. Unlike most other sports or hobbies, martial arts is pro-gressive. The lessons build on one another.
3. Martial arts is holistic. It encompasses a structure of growth for the mind, body, and spirit. So does this book.

But by no means do you need to sign up at the nearest dojo to achieve your black belt in badassery. This book is meant for women of all ages and athletic ability because the lessons it teaches are about inner strength, not punching and kicking. In fact, the original purpose of martial arts training was not to strike first, strike hard, and have no mercy, like Cobra Kai. The real purpose was to develop the whole person into an empathetic leader and warrior who fights for justice, like Daniel-san in *The Karate Kid.*

Martial artists all start out as white belts, total amateurs. They show up to the dojo every day, dress in uniforms, tie on a crisp white belt, bow deeply, and step onto the mat. On the mat is where they learn new skills and drill them until they're blue in the face. They learn how to get knocked down and pick themselves up again to fight another day. They stretch and become more flexible in body, mind, and spirit. They condition themselves to become stronger in every way. They meditate and become more grounded. They use their voices. They learn to believe in their innate power.

Slowly, they progress from one belt level to the next. From white to yellow to orange to green to blue to red, and, finally, to the black belt: pure mastery. Just when they're confident that they can move from one belt level to the next, they're faced with a hard test. A test of their skills, discipline, and, ultimately, their warrior mindset.

This book is laid out in a linear fashion, similar to the martial artist's journey from white to black belt. As you read it, think of the dojo as a metaphor for life. Stepping onto the mat is where we do the work. The inner skills of a warrior can be learned, practiced, and strengthened. You'll move through different belt levels, explore the lessons, and then internalize each with a "belt test" at the end before you move on to the next level.

Instead of a dojo, your life happens in your home, office, commute, gym, and your favorite bars or restaurants. Instead of sinking your bare feet onto a mat, you're doing your work in your Converse or Jimmy Choos, wearing your favorite uniform, whether it be yoga pants or a pants suit. You're out there sparring with opponents, which may mean wrestling with financial hardships, a difficult boss, or being in a manipulative relationship. You stretching is getting out of your comfort zone. You gain strength because you know how your mind and body are connected. You becoming grounded may be any type of mindfulness practice that makes you feel connected to the earth and humanity.

Your journey to become a black belt in badassery started long ago, the first time you were faced with a challenge, a bully on the playground, or a misogynistic comment. I wrote this book to remind you of how strong you are. You're a fucking tiger, and after reading this book, you'll be able to roar fiercely and unapologetically for what you believe in.

The world needs your power and your voice now. The world needs more women to speak up and stand up to bullshit norms of inequality. The world needs you to take up space and share your gifts, not shrink because someone told you that you weren't good enough. The world needs all of you—the good and the messy. It's time that we rise up together and pull up those who need some extra help along the way. We need you to fill leadership positions in corporations, raise strong and loving children (if you want), lead community organizations, and fill the highest seats in our government bodies.

My greatest wish is that this book will help you realize that all the power you need to accomplish your dreams is already within you. You don't have to go outside yourself searching for it. It won't be found in the latest $100 antiaging face cream, expensive purse, or a number on the bathroom scale. Your power may be muted or drained, but walking through this journey and unleashing your inner badass will help you reclaim and regenerate all of it. Every single drop.

So let's (metaphorically speaking) enter the dojo. Put on a uniform and tie the white belt around your waist. Take a deep bow to honor yourself and your journey to this very moment in time. Now, step onto the mat and let's get to work. Because the world needs our badassery now more than ever. 🏯

CHAPTER ONE

White Belt:
Embrace the Suck

I'll never forget the three powerful words my mom said to me after I cried to her about a terrible breakup. I'd just found out that the man I'd been dating for years had recently had a baby with someone else. He somehow forgot to mention this bit of information, and I might never have known it if I hadn't discovered a letter from the other woman talking about the daughter "we're having together." When I read those words, my mind went blank. I felt shocked, enraged, betrayed, humiliated—all at once. After my initial exorcism and a cooling-off period that involved a lot of tequila, I shared the story with my mom and told her how unfair it was to be treated this way.

Her very straightforward response: "Life isn't fair, Jenn."

Now, you may think this sounds a little harsh or even cold coming from a mom who has just heard about her daughter's heartbreak. But for me it was the most freeing piece of advice that I'd ever been given by anyone.

She was right. Life. Isn't. Fair. Life can be hard and even cruel sometimes, but who are we to expect that life should follow some kind of mandate that we've made up? It's not fair that some babies are born with diseases and others are completely healthy. It's not fair that some people are born into wealthy, privileged families, and others are born into slums or refugee camps. It's not fair that some people get accepted into universities because of family connections over people who truly deserve those spots. When someone takes advantage of your kindness or your generosity, it is not fair. If someone gets the job because of their gender or race, that's not fair either.

Do these things happen all the time with maddening frequency? Sure. Does that make us powerless? Not even a little bit. In fact, letting go of the perception that life should be fair takes away a bit of the bite and a lot of the struggle. It doesn't excuse people's bad behavior, but it gives us the opportunity to take our power back by not getting stuck on the feeling of victimhood or the idea that we're being punished by some unknown force called "life." Instead, we can focus on the fact that shit happens, fair or unfair, and how we deal with it is everything.

As a white belt, you're about to see how those difficult and unfair moments have helped shape you into the person you are today. In this chapter, you'll learn how to get spiritually naked, honor your past, and build proof that you already have a badass warrior inside just waiting to be let out.

What It Means to Be a White Belt

In martial arts, the white belt student has to get used to being uncomfortable. There are a ton of protocols and traditions to learn that must be followed to embark on this new journey. If not followed, there's usually some sort of pain associated with it, like being called out in front of the class or being tasked with an extra set of push-ups.

Upon entering the dojo, there's a sense of stripping down to the basics right away. First, shoes are left at the door as all training is done in bare feet. Street clothes are taken off and jewelry and makeup removed; even wearing perfume is considered offensive. A clean, white, boxy uniform that makes all bodies look similar is the only option for clothing. Then one learns to tie their white belt around their waist in a slow, methodical way, preparing for the mental battle that's coming.

Next comes the bowing as a sign of respect. It's done upon entering and leaving the dojo at the beginning and end of class to pretty much anyone who is a higher rank (which, as a white belt, is just about everyone). It's a lot of bowing. And all this is just in preparation for getting onto the mat in the first place.

On the mat is where the discomfort really begins. At first, the main source of pain has little to do with someone else inflicting it. As a white belt, the pain usually comes from getting the mind and body to do things it's not used to doing. Punching, kicking, stretching. If the muscles aren't used to this kind of work, they are going to be SORE and uncomfortable until the body starts to adapt. But the good news is that muscles break down and build back even stronger with every push-up, plank, and squat.

Life is similar. We get pushed and pulled and punched and kicked. We get banged up and bruised and stretched to our limits. And little by little we adapt to the uncomfortable, which stretches our capacity for uncomfortable experiences even further. The more we stretch, the greater our range of experience becomes. If you want to live a badass life, you're going to need to allow for a wide range of experiences—good, bad, amazing, and disastrous.

Stepping into the dojo and tying on that white belt is a symbol, an acknowledgment to yourself and to others that you're willing to embrace the suck, whatever that may be. And embracing the suck is about admitting to yourself that terrible things have happened and are going to continue to happen in life. That doesn't mean reconciling yourself to being smacked down and staying there because there's nothing you can do about it. It doesn't mean burying your head in the positive-affirmation sand and wishing the suck would just go away. It means embracing the smackdowns as opportunities to learn what you're capable of, to practice getting back up again, and to remind yourself that you have the inner strength to do so, even when you're not sure how.

When you can do that, when you can really embrace the suck, then you can stop wasting energy on protesting life's unfairness, wishing things were different, or blaming others or yourself for what went wrong. You will have more energy to focus on building strength and making things better. And the more you do it, the easier it becomes to bounce back after the next hard fall or big fat failure. Because you've exercised those muscles already, they'll be there when you need them.

Getting Naked

After the events of September 11, I became a personal trainer. I would spend hours going in and out of the New York City subways and walking the city streets past the fish markets of Chinatown for one client appointment and fancy brownstones in the West Village for the next. At the same time I was navigating the city's terrain, I was also having to navigate my clients' personalities, all extremely different. For the tough, extremely successful woman who wanted to be pushed to her physical limits, I had to be tougher and almost militant in my style, or else she would try to bully me. For the real estate mogul who just wanted to talk about his dating escapades and financial investments, I had to be funny and interesting. For the famous actress who would bribe me to go get a beer and a soft-shell crab sandwich with her rather than train her, I had to be the perfect mix of focused and flexible.

When I finally got to the dojo at the end of my workday, I was ready to train. But first, I had to get spiritually naked, back to the core of who I am. Off came my shoes, and with them the stress of the hustle and bustle would start to melt away. As I washed the makeup off my face, the personas I took on to accommodate others dissolved. I released any desire to please the outside world with my appearance as I changed out of my clothes and into my uniform. The practice of tying my belt around my waist was like a meditation that brought me solidly into the present moment. The whiteness of my belt symbolized a clean slate and a beginner's mind: open and ready to learn. I knew the next few hours would be challenging to my whole being but that I could handle any challenge sent my way. When I was ready, I would take a deep breath and step onto the mat, feeling my feet sink into the rubbery surface, solidifying the connection of my mind and body.

When we are being challenged in life, we often build up armor so we can avoid pain. We bury ourselves in work, we make jokes to distract from the depth of the situation, we take on self-destructive habits that numb us, or we binge on Netflix and takeout. Our coping mechanisms become our suits of armor.

Embracing the suck means having the courage to examine the armor you use to get through difficult times. Doing so will give you the opportunity to strip down and get a bit naked so you can see who you truly are at your core—who you've always been since before you were hurt, betrayed, or disappointed. Because here's the thing about armor: you put it on because it helps to keep you safe, for a time. It's useful to avoid a painful past or a challenging period, but after a while it starts to weigh heavily on you. It gets in the way of forming deep relationships or going after your dream career or lifestyle. When it's stripped away, what's left is authentically you. The purest essence of who you are without the hard shell separating you from the world around you. That "you" has limitless potential and the heart of a warrior. She can stay open and present and eventually bounce back from drama, trauma, or tragedy.

When going through difficult times, people typically use some form of the following as armor:

- **Defensiveness:** Fighting or acting aggressively in the face of adversity

- **Denial:** Pretending like the situation isn't as challenging as it is or denying the impact it's having on you or others

- **Fixing:** Wanting to make things better for everyone even if it winds up taking a toll on you or worsening the situation

- **Numbing:** Using alcohol, drugs, food, social media, video games, TV, or burying yourself in work in an unhealthy way as escapism from reality

- **Running away:** Avoiding or fleeing the situation whenever possible

- **Deflecting:** Using comedy or sarcasm to pretend like the situation isn't affecting you

Sometimes we use just one dominant form of armor and sometimes we use multiple forms. For example, after I found out about my ex's secret baby, I built up some serious layers of armor. I was angry. I mean, really angry. As soon as I read that letter, I flew into a fit of rage. As if I were in a scene from *Sex and the City,* I ran out of his office, onto the street, and headed straight for the nearest Staples store. Something inside me said that I needed proof of what I had just learned because nobody would believe me. So, I proceeded to print tons of copies of this letter. Unlike Samantha Jones, I never posted them for the world to see, but I felt safer having them as evidence for whatever was to come next.

Over the next weeks and even months, I numbed with daily doses of alcohol, and I even went through times of denial. Not denial of the facts per se, but denial of my values and true desires. I had moments of believing that we could build back our relationship even stronger, even though deep inside I didn't want to. I mean, HE HAD A BABY WITH SOMEONE ELSE AND DIDN'T TELL ME! I knew he wasn't capable of being the partner I really wanted in life, but I would try to convince myself that maybe he was. Luckily, I was terrible at denial, and ultimately knew that, for my own good, I needed to drop this armor and get back to my core.

I distanced myself from him as much as possible and was finally able to let down the armor. Over time, I was able to release most of the anger that I felt from the betrayal and move on with my life. I came back to my core, back to who I was and what I wanted to be for others before I was betrayed, which was open, loving, and even trusting of the good in others. Then I was able to get clear on what I really wanted in my next relationship.

Identifying the armor I was using has helped me realize when I start to pick it back up again. Getting defensive when I feel like someone may want to take advantage of me is really useful in the moment. It allows me to stick up for myself when there is unfairness and deal with the issue at hand. However, I don't want to hold onto that armor and bring it into every interaction I have going forward. Using defensiveness in all your interactions makes it feel like there are always people out to harm you and it definitely doesn't allow for making deep connections.

Using armor with discernment and intention is how we take our power back from situations that sucked in our lives. When we choose the armor we use versus the armor choosing us, that is when we have more control. We can pick it up to protect us and put it down when we know it is no longer useful. The following are some examples of how to use discernment when choosing your armor.

Defensiveness: Anger can be a very helpful tool to cope with situations where you feel sad, hurt, and vulnerable. If someone has lied to you or tried to take advantage of you, anger can be used to motivate you to change the situation, either by removing that person from your life or confronting them and their actions toward you. However, when you hold onto anger for too long, it can turn into bitterness and resentment, which only winds up hurting you.

Denial: Denial of facts or denial of your values can be helpful in the short term to get you through a difficult situation like a betrayal or breakup when the reality feels too heavy to hold. But sooner or later, you're going to have to face the music if you want to move forward.

Fixing: Fixing situations can make you feel really good, like the hero of a movie. Fixing other people's problems or saving the day with a much-needed chunk of money or act of service can give you a blast of dopamine. But when your desire to fix problems becomes all-consuming and you no longer take care of your own life and your goals fall by the wayside, it's time to hold off on being Superwoman and examine how you can strike a better balance of self-care and superhero.

Numbing: There's a big difference between having a glass of wine or two at dinner with friends or family versus drinking a bottle of wine by yourself to deal with a divorce or a job search. The latter doesn't help you move forward in life. It's used to numb feelings of loss or stress. When the booze (or Netflix, or drugs, or video games, or fill in the blank) takes a toll on your health and motivation, it's time to take a look at putting that armor down.

Running away: Running from a difficult situation can be helpful, like if you ever find yourself in an abusive relationship with a partner or boss. But when running from uncomfortable situations is your MO, it can be difficult to feel settled down and safe in your own skin. If you're in danger, run. If you're not, perhaps take a look at why your urge is to keep running away from challenges.

Deflecting: I love humor. I love funny people. I can also tell the difference between someone who's making a joke to make others laugh and making a joke at their own expense to cover up or deflect their feelings of disappointment or despair. Again, using humor to deflect from a difficult situation can be useful, and it can feel really good to bring a smile to someone's face. However, if you always deflect and never get real with your emotions, it's basically the same as denial. You won't be able to process the challenges of your past or present and get to the part where you can make peace with yourself and warrior on.

Exercise: Getting Naked

Let's take a look at the armor you may have been using by default all this time. Take out your favorite notebook and a pen. Consider the following prompts and write down, without judgment, whatever comes to mind.

The most important thing here is to practice nonjudgment. None of these behaviors make you a bad person for doing them. They are simply the best armor that you took on at the time. This is an exercise to uncover the behaviors you've been using to mask your hurt, disappointment, or feelings of unworthiness.

1. Name a difficult situation you're facing now. Then ask yourself:
   - Are you very defensive and confrontational when it comes to the situation and other areas in your life?
   - Are you trying to pretend like it's not happening?
   - Are you going out of your way to placate others, fix the

situation, or act in a way that feels completely inauthentic to you?

- Are you developing brain-numbing habits like scrolling Instagram for hours or binging on Netflix?
- Are you using food as a way to try to numb out or feel control?
- Are you overdoing the vino as a way to take the edge off?
- Are you burying yourself in work to avoid the issue?
- Have you left the situation completely without really dealing with it?
- Do you use humor as a tool to distract from the seriousness of the situation?
- What if you didn't use these behaviors as armor? How might things be different?
- Without that armor, who are you at your core?
- What are your personality traits that you love and value the most about yourself? Name at least three.

2. Choose more difficult situations from your past and follow the same prompts.

3. To complete the exercise, review your previous answers. Do you notice any patterns? Have you been using the same armor time and time again? If so, did you go far enough into your past to see where and when you started using it?

Does the armor that you decided to use as a young girl or teenager serve you as the woman you are today? If not, it might be time to stop carrying around that heavy suit. Maybe not all at once, but little by little. Slowly get naked, back to the core of who you really are.

Bowing to Your Past

Now that you've gotten a little naked and had some time to uncover all the kick-ass things that make you YOU, let's continue to embrace the suck. You just started to look back into your past to find out why you behave the way you do, and now it's time to honor yourself with a deep bow. When was the last time you honored yourself for how far you've come? From that tiny girl you used to be to the fierce woman you've grown into. Taking a moment to honor your path mentally prepares you to appreciate the bumps in the road instead of resenting them.

A quick review of your history can give you some insight into what a powerful warrior you already are. I bet you've already walked through some heart-wrenching, soul-crushing fires and developed some serious mental muscles. In fact, your journey to black belt began with the first harsh words you endured or the annoying bully on the playground who decided to mess with you.

Think of times in your past when you've had to deal with judgments, bullies, failures, disappointments, or even traumas. As awful as they were, can you see how they made you stronger? How they stretched your capacity for handling life? Good, bad, amazing, awful?

After losing my dad to prostate cancer right before my wedding and my fortieth birthday, I was left shell-shocked and devastated. Dad was my rock and my biggest cheerleader. He was also a pinnacle example of health and fitness for men in their seventies, which was why nobody saw his illness coming. But there I was, six months before he was supposed to walk me down the aisle, saying goodbye to his body in the hospital.

I don't think you ever truly get over a loss of that magnitude, but in the last few years I can see how that suffering has made me more empathetic. I can see how it has expanded my capacity for handling disappointments, like my first, and even my third pregnancy loss. They didn't crush me as badly as they might have if they had been the first major losses I suffered. I experienced the loss, and it reminded me that I've been down this road of disappointment and grief before in a major way. I knew I had the capacity to get through it again. As corny as it sounds, the old adage does ring true: What doesn't kill you makes you stronger. Not in the moment or even during the season of suck, but you do gain strength once you emerge from it if you can allow yourself to honor your past instead of being a victim to it.

Honoring your past is important to build proof of your strength. You've gone through really shit times before and you've emerged alive and here to tell the tale. You've also accomplished really awesome and difficult things. Let's take a walk down memory lane and remember how strong you are by creating your Greatest (S)hits Lists and your Greatest Hits List.

Exercise: Your Greatest (S)hits List

Every heartache, disappointment, failure, and blow to your confidence has contributed to your current level of badassery. You survived. You emerged from the muck. You're in one piece. Go, you!

What's more, you've grown as a result. You've learned and you've developed strength. Let's take some time to acknowledge and honor that by creating your Greatest (S)hits List.

After taking my client Katie through this exercise, she said, "I realized that shitty experiences that feel dramatic and all-consuming in the moment really do evolve and fade with time. This exercise was extremely empowering."

To create your Greatest (S)hits Lists, we're going to head back to your childhood and look for any disappointments, feelings of shame and embarrassment, and perceived failures. We'll start there and write each one down as we move through your herstory to the present day.

This is an important step in stripping down and confronting what makes you unique. It's not about what you look like or the clothes you wear. It's not about what you do for a living or what you post on social media. It's what you've been through that matters most. And some of those experiences may be hard to talk about, which is why we're simply writing them down. No judgment. No regrets. For no one to read but us. And then, in the next section, you'll get to see how you've become stronger with each one.

1. Take out your journal and favorite pen.
2. Close your eyes and visualize a timeline in front of you. This is a timeline of your life from your first day on Earth until the present moment. Imagine yourself floating above your timeline and looking back at your past. Begin to bring to mind moments or seasons in your life that absolutely sucked.
3. Watch the scenes play out just as if you were watching a movie of your life. Stay as the observer of the movie as you float above it; you don't want to get bogged down in the old emotions of your past.
4. Turn the movie you are watching into a black and white so

it feels even more distant and in the past. As you watch one scene of the sucky movie, keep going back into your past to look for more and more. When you finally have recalled as many as you can, go ahead and float back to your present moment and come into your body again. Open your eyes.

5. Now take your pen and write down all the shitty memories you have.

Remember there is no judgment needed; this is just a list of facts from the past. We will be using it in the next exercise to fully grasp the breadth of your badassery.

> **Examples from Jenn's Greatest (S)hits List**
> - Almost dying on September 11, 2001
> - Getting attacked by some creep on the street one night
> - Ghosted by a guy I thought I had a great connection with
> - Being betrayed by my old boyfriend who had a baby with someone else
> - Being fired by a client after I asked for a retainer
> - Getting fired from a reality TV show
> - My dad's unexpected and tragic death
> - Harsh criticism after a speaking gig
> - My first, second, and third pregnancy losses

Finding Your Secret Weapons

Is anyone else sick of hearing whiny celebrities tell us that we're not broken? No shit. Of course, we're not broken. Women cannot break. Maybe we've picked up some extra wrinkles and gray hairs along the way, but we certainly don't combust under pressure. If anything, we're like diamonds formed under times of high heat and intense pressure. Each carat that forms represents unique powers that we can shine onto the world.

Your Secret Weapons were formed under times of high heat and intense pressure. They aren't traits that you were born with, like your natural hair color or the shape of your thighs. They have nothing to do with your appearance and everything to do with your spirit. They are what set you apart from the crowd and allow you to rise above the noise.

Your Secret Weapons have helped you navigate difficult relationships, make better choices, connect with people on deeper levels, and perhaps contribute to humanity with some cool-ass ideas of your own. Your Secret Weapons couldn't be learned in school and there's no certification program to earn them. You earn them at the School of Hard Knocks, most times in ways you NEVER asked for, NEVER wanted, and NEVER deserved. Following are some examples of Secret Weapons and how they were developed:

Empathy: Losing a loved one has now made you the most empathetic love bug to anyone going through grief. You're the first to drop off warm cookies, and you're the shoulder people can cry on.

Generosity: Growing up poor sucked at the time but has motivated you to earn loads of cash and to be generous to those who are less fortunate.

Humility: You built a business and it failed miserably. You didn't give up and instead you developed humility as you tried again. People think of you as a humble leader.

Independence: Your parents divorced when you were young, and you were fast-tracked into learning self-sufficiency while Mom or Dad had to work. Your independence has helped you succeed at getting shit done!

Intuition: Being betrayed by someone you trusted has supercharged your bullshit meter and your intuition has skyrocketed. You can spot danger and deceit before anyone else.

Balance: You worked yourself into exhaustion. You were physically tired, mentally drained, and perhaps your once vibrant health came to a screeching halt. You learned to prioritize yourself and your well-being by managing your time and adopting a healthier work/life balance.

Flexibility: You planned every meticulous detail of your life. When you wanted to get married. To whom. Your dress. The ceremony. When you'd buy your first home. When you would have children. Ha! Life doesn't always go as planned. There was a major hitch in your plans and you learned that you could be more flexible and not so attached to the perfect outcome.

Resilience: You've landed on your butt more times than you can count. You've been let go from your job, you've overcome an illness or you live with one, or you've been through a failed relationship. Yet you always land on your feet. Resilience is now part of who you are and because of that you're more willing to take risks in life.

Perseverance: You were an athlete and you always set a high bar for yourself. Also, you experienced setbacks along the way, perhaps injuries or fierce competition. Your goals always outweighed your challenges and you learned how to persevere. You now take that Secret Weapon into your career, health, and relationships.

Exercise: Moving from Shit List to Secret Weapons

Andrea, who took my Embrace the Suck workshop and created her Greatest (S)hits List, found her Secret Weapons of resilience and flexibility and said, "It was so helpful to turn difficult, horrible, and embarrassing memories into powerful tools in a tangible way. I don't know that I'll ever look at those shitty experiences the same way again. What a relief!"

Now you! Head right back to your Greatest (S)hits List, and for each entry spend some time with the memory. Remember how difficult it felt while you were going through it and then think of the you that emerged. Here are a few questions to ask yourself:

• What did I learn about myself from the experience?

• What skills did I gain as a result?

• How have I turned the experience into a positive for myself or another person?

Write down all the Secret Weapons that come to mind. Looking back as an observer, see how your experience has helped you become stronger, more empathetic, more determined, more generous, or whatever Secret Weapons have emerged for you. Tip: I have my Secret Weapons written on Post-it Notes and they are stuck around my office as reminders.

These weapons are your greatest assets, and you may not have developed them if it weren't for that (S)hit List of yours. The next time you are faced with a challenge, from interviewing for a job that you really want to starting your side hustle candle-making business, lean into these weapons of yours. Arm yourself with them wherever you go and pull them out when needed. You've earned them and now they are here to serve you and perhaps others. Can you see where they've already been helpful to you in your life? If so, maybe, just maybe, you can look back at that list and find a tiny bit of gratitude for the nitty-gritty times, even though they sucked.

Being thankful for shit times is not easy and I don't expect you to celebrate them. But you can (if you want) be grateful for who they have helped shape you into today. The next exercise will help you remember all the kick-ass things you've done with the help of your Secret Weapons.

Your Greatest Hits List

When life knocks us out, it's easy to forget how far we've come. Your business fails, you lose a sale, or your partner dumps you, and suddenly you're a puddle on the floor. But I know you: You've accomplished epic shit before and that's just proof that you can do epic shit again.

When we're feeling like a failure, loser, or whatever horrible word we're using to describe ourselves, our brain looks for evidence to back that up. It will start to pull memories of all the times that you did fail at your work, your relationships, or your attempts at a fitness goal. It will say, "Look, look, you are a loser. Remember the time when {fill in the blank with all those perceived failures}." It makes you feel like crap, and if you're not careful, it can lead to a downward spiral of ugly self-loathing.

Your Greatest Hits List is an intervention to that downward spiral. It's a tool to shift your brain into remembering all your past achievements. When you start focusing on your achievements rather than your failures, you start to feel good, and good is better than crap. The more you focus on the memories of those achievements, the more you can start to access those feelings of confidence, strength, and badassery. Then you can take those feelings, which are powerful mental states, into whatever challenge you currently face.

Your (S)hits List was about what you've endured; now we're going to focus on how you've kicked ass. There are surely times when you've felt on top of the world, and that's worth dwelling on.

I have all my clients create a Greatest Hits List, a compilation of all their epic achievements on paper. This way, when they come to me with a challenge they're facing, I can have them go back to their list and remember times when they have achieved things much more difficult and scarier than the thing they are worried about currently. This gives them the confidence to tackle the current problem with grace and confidence or go after future goals with gusto.

When my client Sofia wanted to raise her rates for her coaching practice, she was so nervous she would offend her current clients and lose them in the process. After creating her Greatest Hits List, Sofia was able to tap into the same confident state that helped her open her practice in the first place. She realized she had already raised her rates once before (going from zero to her first paying client), so she could absolutely do it again. And guess what? Not one client left her practice.

When I was starting out as a public speaker, I would get

so nervous before my events. The night before a big event was always the worst. I would pace inside my hotel room and get so nervous that I would stop preparing for my talk altogether and instead binge-watch bad TV shows and order room service. The only thing that helped me break the habit was to write down my Greatest Hits List. I would remember each time that I had spoken in front of a large group before. Even if it wasn't as large, it was still getting up in front of a crowd. I would remember the feeling of accomplishment when I would walk off those stages and feel those feelings again. My mind would begin to say, "Oh yeah, I've done this before and that's just proof that I can do it again." Then I would start to relax, prepare for my talk, and step out onstage the next day with the confidence and poise of a professional speaker.

Making the connection from the event on your Greatest Hits List to the thing you're currently worried about doesn't have to be so direct. What you're looking for are times when you've felt confident, powerful, and like a total badass. Then you can link that feeling to the current situation. For example, perhaps you get word that your company is about to do a round of layoffs, and you're not so confident that you won't be in the line of fire. It keeps you up at night worrying what you'll do next and how you'll pay your bills in the meantime. In your Greatest Hits List, there are times when you've kicked the winning goal at a soccer game, asked out a guy you wanted to date, or got an award for your kick-ass performance in a play. You did that! Remember how amazing it felt. Of course, you can withstand the current uncertainty of your job. You can do difficult things.

Now let's see all the awesome things you've done. It's time to create your Greatest Hits List. Take out your favorite pen and a journal. Take a look into your past and remember the times that you accomplished amazing things. Start to create a list of all the times you felt proud of your achievements. Here are some prompts to get you started:

- Did you ace a really hard test?
- Have you graduated from high school, college, or a graduate program?
- Did you ever nail an interview?
- Have you gotten the dream job?
- Have you asked for a raise or promotion that you deserved and received it?
- Have you made a huge sale or started a business or a side hustle?
- Have you ever received a large check for your hard work?
- Have you ever swiped right, made the first move, or solidified a commitment with your dream partner?
- Have you ever traveled somewhere on your bucket list?
- Have you ever jumped out of an airplane or done some other wacky adrenaline-pumping feat?
- Have you ever given a praiseworthy presentation that you were really nervous about?
- Have you ever crushed an athletic goal like a race, a workout of the day, or a dance performance?

Once you have your list (and you can always go back to it to add more), sit and stare at it. Take it all in from the perspective of an observer. Observe all these achievements and think about what kind of person it takes to accomplish all these feats. Perhaps it would take the kind of person who has all those Secret Weapons that you discovered as ammo? As the observer, can you feel really proud of this person? If you're able to feel proud as the observer, now take those same feelings and give them to yourself. Soak them in and start to feel them filling up your spirit. You deserve them. You've done difficult things, and you can and you will do them again.

A Note If You're Currently in the Suck . . .

If you are in the suck right now, I'm not telling you to get over it as quickly as possible and move on with your life. Feeling the pain and discomfort of an experience is a necessary part of moving through it. Completing the exercises in this chapter and your upcoming white belt test won't make them go away or miraculously heal you overnight. Unleashing your inner black belt takes time and continuous practice.

When you allow yourself to feel anger, hurt, sadness, anxiousness, and even depression, you allow yourself time for healing. It's a completely normal part of life to go through these stages of emotional healing. For some reason, society would have us believe that we need to get over things quickly instead of sit in the shit for a while. However, when giving yourself time, it's helpful to also give yourself parameters so you don't spiral into the dark abyss.

As I said earlier, embracing the suck isn't about wishing it away, pretending it never happened, or wallowing in it. It's an active process of allowing feelings to come and go and taking time for loads of self-reflection. Then you can use the exercises in this chapter as mini-interventions to keep your head above water and eventually walk one foot in front of the other back to shore.

Personally, I like to give myself parameters for sitting in the shit. During times of intense stress or sadness, I am aware when I start to spiral downward. When one negative thought leads to another and another and suddenly my mind is telling me I'm a giant failure and I need to run away to a cabin in the woods and raise bees for the rest of time. (Note: If you are a beekeeper, I have the ultimate respect for you. I don't think of beekeeping as failing but more as retreating from my real life.)

Instead of letting my mind torture myself with negativity for hours, I'll put a time limit on it. I'll say to myself that I have ten minutes to feel these miserable feelings and then I must do something that will change my negative state to a more positive one. I pick one intervention from the list that I've compiled that includes:

- Reading my Secret Weapons List and remembering all the inner strength I've gained

- Reading my Greatest Hits List and feeling the feelings of my greatest accomplishments

- Getting outside for a brisk walk down to the ocean and back

- Lifting weights

- Feeling gratitude for all I have in my life, starting with my cats, my husband, my family, and my health

- Sitting in meditation and going inward to listen to my higher self

Without fail, these interventions work for me every single time.

Now you're going to create your own Intervention List of ideas that will help you stop the negative spiral when you're going through hard times. Go back to your journal, or you can write in the spaces below. It doesn't have to be a long list, just a few items will do. And you already have some from this chapter! What are a few other things that you like to do that change your state immediately? Play with your kids? Pet your pup? Practice yoga?

1. Read your Secret Weapons List.
2. Read your Greatest Hits List and feel the feelings of your accomplishments.
3.
4.
5.

Sometimes the circumstances of what you're going through feel too heavy to carry by yourself. Sometimes you just feel like you're drowning. If that is the case, get help. Reach out to friends and family and tell them how you're feeling. Enlist the counsel of a therapist, perhaps someone in your religious practice or a counselor who is trained to help people through difficult times. You do not have to do this alone. It's not a bother to ask people for help. People love helping people, the emotionally intelligent ones, anyway. And there is NO shame in the therapy game. Period.

Once you've completed the exercises in this chapter, it's time for your first belt test. Your challenges have not been in vain. Yes, they sucked. But there's no point in resenting them or wishing to change the past. The past is unchangeable, and the only empowering thing we can do is embrace it and move on. We'll conclude the chapter (and all chapters) with a belt test.

Belt tests are a symbol of accomplishment and forward movement. It's not about winning or losing; it's about testing the skills you've learned and honoring your progression. I highly suggest you set aside some time for yourself to complete each one before moving on to the next chapter.

Belt Test: White to Yellow (#badassbelttest)

PREPARE YOURSELF

1. If possible, set up in a room that you have all to yourself. Clear some space on the floor. Dim the lights, light a candle, burn some sage, play some peaceful music, or do whatever it is you like to make your space feel sacred. If it feels good and not too kooky, remove your makeup, jewelry, and fancy clothes. Put on something that feels like you're stripping down to the basics: a robe, your favorite PJs, or just a monotone outfit of yoga pants and your favorite tee.

2. Have your Greatest (S)hits List and your Greatest Hits List out and ready.

3. Step onto the mat. The mat can be a designated area in a room you deem fit for introspection.

START YOUR TEST

1. Beginning with your Greatest (S)hits List, read each entry out loud, starting with the oldest entry first.

2. For each entry, reflect on how far you've come since it happened. Honor yourself for your resilience and inner strength by taking a deep bow and stepping forward to

symbolize your unique journey.

A note on bowing: A respectful bow is done carefully and slowly. Hands are placed at your side or in front of your chest in a prayer position. Bend at your hips, keeping your back flat. Bend at least 45 degrees, or to 90 degrees if you can, and lower your eyes to the floor.

3. Continue doing the same for each entry. When you've finished the list, look behind you and see how far you've come from where your journey began.

4. Now take your Greatest Hits List and do the same. Read each entry out loud and reflect on your inner strength. Relive each experience in your mind and feel the accomplishment, confidence, and strength in your mind, body, and spirit. Complete each entry with a deep bow of respect to yourself and your bravery.

Congratulations! You've embraced the suck. You're now a yellow belt and one step closer to being a full-blown black belt in badassery. Feel free to share your results with a post or a pic after each test using the hashtag #badassbelttest. 🏯

CHAPTER TWO

Yellow Belt: Bounce Back

After September 11, 2001, I made some major moves. I lost my job as an event planner before I even got to plan any events, and my career came to a screeching halt. I was still scarred with a side of PTSD, but I decided that, somehow, I was going to follow my martial arts and create a meaningful new career.

In that same year, as I was walking to my apartment late one night, I was grabbed on the street by some creep. In a flash, his hands were up my dress. I flew around to face him and went into full beast mode. Flailing my arms, making myself larger than life, and yelling in the deepest voice I had, I was able to scare him off. As he fled from me, I chased him down the street, still wearing my favorite black stilettos.

After that incident, I got really serious about my self-defense training. I trained longer and harder than before and started to practice better awareness when I was out and about. Eight years later, I moved to Los Angeles and started teaching women's self-defense workshops that I named "Stilettos and Self Defense," as a nod to that night on the street. Due to the marketing hook, I wound up getting booked on the local Los Angeles NBC news to tell my story of how Stilettos and Self Defense came to be.

A few days after that I got an e-mail from a booker at the *Today* show who had seen the local NBC spot. If you knew me then, you would know that my mornings consisted of training my clients and rushing back home to catch Kathie Lee and Hoda Kotb drink their Chardonnay with a warm cup of coffee in my hand. So you can imagine my excitement to see an e-mail asking me to call the head booker for the fourth hour of the *Today* show. They flew me from Los Angeles to New York City to teach a Stilettos and Self Defense segment with Hoda Kotb and Carrie Fisher (Kathie Lee was out that day). ARE YOU KIDDING ME? Teach Princess Leia herself to kick butt while wearing her favorite shoes? And when she paused as she was woman-handling my attacker-for-hire to say, "Am I kicking you in the balls first?" I nearly died and went to career highlight heaven.

Instead of September 11 and a near assault on the street stopping me in my tracks, I gave myself time to embrace the suck and then I allowed those sucky experiences to motivate me to explore my passions and create a fulfilling new life. As a yellow belt, you'll come to realize that setbacks and failures don't have to define you. But they can be an opportunity to rise from the ashes like a badass phoenix!

What It Means to Be a Yellow Belt

A yellow belt in martial arts begins to learn footwork drills to be able to move out of their opponent's way or to change direction quickly. They learn mat work, which is essentially how to fall down and get back up again as quickly as possible. A lot of people start training because they want to be able to take someone down or kick someone's ass. They're sometimes surprised to learn that the emphasis in the beginning is on just the opposite. You've got to know how to get back on your feet before you can ever hope to win a fight.

In order to live a life of badassery, you're going to need to put yourself out there, on the mat, with other people. You're going to have to try new things and be willing to fail. You'll have to learn how to deal with difficult situations and even more difficult people. The bottom line is, you're going to have stuff thrown at you, time and time again. Sometimes you're even going to get knocked down.

When that happens, you have choices. You can simply give up on living the life of your dreams, resigned to the thought that life is too hard, so you'll just hide out and play small for the rest of time. Or you can take a pause and change direction by learning the art of the pivot. You can roll with the punches or even choose to make an epic comeback like Madonna or Rocky Balboa. Which option sounds better to you?

Five Rules of Resiliency

Yellow belt level is all about resiliency. It's about knowing how to take a punch and recover. It's about knowing how to avoid some of the punches in the first place so you don't have to spend so much time and effort recovering. Let's jump into learning the rules of resiliency, five simple things that will help us gain the perspective needed to be resilient.

1. It's a season, not a life sentence

You failed the entrance exam but that doesn't mean you're going to fail every test you're ever going to take in life. You didn't get the job you wanted, but that doesn't mean you're never going to have a job you love. Your business idea never took off, but that doesn't mean you'll never have a successful business. Your grandparent that you adored passed away, but that doesn't mean you'll be this sad every day for the rest of your life. Things that seem all-consuming and terrible usually fade with time.

Life has seasons, and winter doesn't last forever. (Unless you live in the Arctic and if you do, get the hell out of the Arctic.) Eventually, spring and summer come along with longer days of sunshine and brightness. If you think of your life as cyclical, it will give you a deeper perspective on experiencing dark days. They're necessary in order to experience the light.

2. Bad things sometimes happen to good people

Sure, karma's a bitch . . . if you did something terrible on purpose. But believing in a simplified version of karma as the key principle of why bad things happen to people is seriously flawed. Sometimes shit happens to the best of us when we've done nothing wrong in this life to deserve it. This goes back to my earlier point that life isn't always fair. There's nothing we can do to change that, so accepting it is the only way forward.

This is especially important to remember when you start to think that you deserve all the crap that's happening to you. There's a difference between taking responsibility for your life and blaming yourself for things outside your control. Taking responsibility for what you have contributed to the failures = good; blaming yourself = a waste of time and energy. Use that energy instead to figure out how to bounce back from the crap.

3. Hurt people, hurt people

This is a tough one. It really is. But the reality is that emotionally stable, well-adjusted people usually don't go around hurting other people. When people hurt people, they are usually playing out some old wound from their past.

The guy who cheated on you. The person who stole from you. The jerk on the street who scared you. It's easy to blame a bully for being an asshole. It's more difficult to see the person as someone who's been hurt in the past and is acting out old wounds. Having empathy for a bully, even just a little bit, can allow us to imagine that maybe the act against us wasn't entirely personal. And that gives us a window for moving past it.

If empathy is too big of a stretch, not taking things so personally is a way to take our power back from a terrible situation. Is there a time in your life when someone hurt you and you still haven't gotten over it? Over time, that resentment is like acid, rotting away at your happiness and positivity. That resentment is energy, energy that could be used on things that you want for your life, like a supportive partner or a successful career.

Just for a moment, imagine that the act really had nothing to do with you. That the person who hurt you was acting out from a painful childhood and somehow thought that hurting someone else would take away their pain. How tragic is that? It doesn't make that person less of a jerk, but does it open up a little more freedom for you? Can it make you less angry, ashamed, or resentful? That bit of space is where freedom lies, and freedom from negative emotions equals power. Power to take on living the life of your dreams.

4. It can always be worse

Ick. I hate saying this because it sounds so cliché. And sometimes it can feel a little gross because you're actually comparing your situation to someone who's had it worse than you. But isn't it kinda true? The situation that you're faced with right now that is consuming your thoughts could actually be worse than it really is.

Your life with your particular set of challenges could actually be someone else's dream life. Isn't that wild to think about? If you're thinking right now that nobody would want your problems, think of someone somewhere in the world that truly has it worse than you. And remember that on your worst day, there is someone somewhere that would trade their problems with yours in a heartbeat.

5. You have choices

Nobody has to be a victim for life. I have seen people heal themselves from trauma, drama, and complete devastation. I have been awestruck by people's resilience in life, and we've all seen stories of how the human spirit can overcome. At the end of the day, it all boils down to mindset. There are people that choose to live with a victim mentality, and there are those who choose to survive and even thrive.

When I start to feel like my problems are piling up and I get a case of the Why Me's? I remind myself of all the people who have inspired me over the years with their resilience. I remember I have a choice in the way I want to think about my challenges. And choice equals more freedom, and freedom equals power.

A victim is someone who has withstood a horrible act against them, from sexual assault to cancer. A victim mentality is a mindset that keeps people stuck. People who keep a victim mentality believe that life is happening to them and not for them and that any moment they may again be victimized. Holding onto this mentality is a way in which we give our power away to people, places, or things that do not deserve it. Shifting to a survivor mentality is a way in which we reclaim our power. Try both on and see how they feel:

- "I am a victim of {fill in the blank}."
- "I survived {fill in the blank}."

Which one feels better in your body? Which one gives you a more positive outlook for your future? Which one feels like you are more resilient than you ever could have imagined? Choose that one.

The Art of the Pivot

Of course, it's one thing to know the rules. It's another to turn them into actions that will support your resiliency. That's where strategies come in. Pivoting is a great strategy on the mat and in life. It helps you change direction quickly after someone or something has tried to knock you down. Without a pivot, you leave yourself open to a life of stagnation. Or worse, you resign yourself to staying on the ground, writhing in pain, defeated.

As I write this, the COVID-19 pandemic has swept the entire globe, paralyzing businesses and forcing some to shutter their doors, while others have chosen to pivot. Some brands have changed their messaging, and others have changed direction in their actual production lines. Fashion brands are now making masks. Car manufacturers are making ventilators. Offices have sent their employees to work from home and made Zoom a household name.

When the lockdown of March 2020 began, I started to hear from my clients regarding my upcoming speaking events: "Postponed until further notice." Cancelled. One by one, my entire year of income completely dried up. I allowed myself to panic for a week or two, but I quickly pivoted. I knew that I had to get creative and fast. Having a year with no income was not an option for me.

I began offering virtual happy hours to foster community and create a space where people could feel connected during chaos. Then I began offering group coaching programs and virtual workshops. I got tons of practice presenting on Zoom early in the pandemic, which set me up to have the best year of my business to date in 2021, mostly online. Prior to the pandemic, I would have never thought I could teach self-defense or give keynotes virtually. Now I'm able to reach hundreds of people spread out all over the globe simultaneously. What an unexpected gift I've received from my pivot.

Pivoting works for businesses as well as it works for individuals. If some aspect of your life is not working, changing direction can look like:

- Changing your romantic partner, because no matter how hard you try you know that this relationship will never work

- Changing direction on your family planning goals by choosing to have or not have children

- Changing your relationship to your body by choosing to stop abusing it with deprivation and dieting and start treating it with respect and admiration

- Changing your financial habits. Stop mindlessly clicking "add to cart," and start socking away money in your 401K to set yourself up for a financially savvy future.

These kinds of pivots can feel big and overwhelming. It can help to practice the art of the pivot in order to develop the skill before applying it to the trickier aspects of our own lives. This is why I'll provide what I call OYH (Out of Your Head) exercises throughout the book. They are an opportunity to move out of your head, where anxiety breeds negative thoughts, and into your body where you can feel strong and powerful. This is an invaluable tool I learned from martial arts. The mat is a safe space where you can feel grounded, stop worrying, and just practice what may (or may not) work for you without anything really being at stake.

OYH Exercise: Footwork (Pivoting)

1. Stand up and separate your feet hip-width apart.

2. Take one walking step forward with your left foot. Keep a slight bend in both your knees. Roll your hands into fists and keep them next to your face. This is called "fighting position."

3. Now turn and face ninety degrees to your right by moving your back foot only. Do this four times until you complete a full circle. Then repeat in the opposite direction.

4. Imagine crap from your life being thrown at you—an insult, a sexually charged comment, bad news—and imagine pivoting out of the way as it flies by you. How does that feel?

Rolling with the Punches

In martial arts we literally learn how to fall. When an opponent knocks you down, you don't want to bash your head on the floor, so we learn to roll with the punches. At first, we learn this technique from a seated position and eventually from standing up. It requires a person to roll backward, as if accepting the impact, and then reverse direction to roll forward again with enough momentum to propel yourself back onto your feet.

Kids are naturals at this. They tuck into tiny balls, roll back and forth, and get right back on their feet in an instant. For adults, it becomes more challenging. We too often get stuck in our heads. We don't trust ourselves to roll backward because we're scared we may not be able to get back up. But once we start trusting ourselves, we learn that we can use the momentum of an impact to our advantage, shifting the direction of the energy in order to stand back up with even more power and velocity.

When you fail at something that means a lot to you, like messing up a client presentation or striking out on getting someone's number, it can feel like a punch to the gut that sends you falling backward, right onto your ass. But the more comfortable you are rolling with the punches, the quicker you can recover. Even if you didn't fail at something, perhaps life just keeps throwing you one huge challenge after another.

Take my friend Emily, for example. On May 4, 2019, Emily and her fiancé's apartment in San Francisco caught on fire. She had just come home from a party, snuggled on the couch with her man, and fell asleep around 1:00 A.M. The fire started in the backyard, and luckily a neighbor noticed it, called the fire department, and banged on their door until they woke up. Then, surrounded by strangers who had all gathered outside to gawk, they watched as their burnt belongings were tossed on the street by the brave firefighters. They lost a lot of stuff, but luckily nobody in the building was hurt. They were able to find a new apartment in a short time.

And the hits kept on coming. Emily's wedding day was planned for October 26, 2019, just five months after the fire episode. Friends and family traveled to wine country in Northern California for a weekend-long celebration of the happy couple's nuptials. At the rehearsal dinner, the week before the wedding, Emily's stepdad choked on a piece of steak so badly that he wound up in the hospital.

Emily made the difficult decision to go forward with the wedding while her stepdad was in a hospital bed. He had now lapsed into a coma.

And the hits kept on coming. Thirty minutes before guests were set to arrive at the wedding venue, the fire marshal arrived on site and told them they must evacuate. With a bit of hustle, luck, and help from her community, Emily was able to relocate the wedding, her vendors, and guests to a friend's home nearby.

And the hits kept on coming. While waiting to board the flight for her honeymoon, she got the call that her stepdad had passed away. Again, with some hustle and good travel insurance, she was able to push her honeymoon back a couple of days, be there for her grieving mom, and eventually head off for her honeymoon with her new husband.

Emily rolled with the punches. When many of us would be overwhelmed with stress and crippling anxiety, she was able to take the hits and roll back on her feet. The most important lesson that she learned throughout the fiery experience was that community is everything. She leaned on them when she needed to. They came to her rescue (just like those hunky firefighters), and they would be there for her anytime she took another leap. Now, that's a powerful lesson.

Here are four strategies to help you roll with the punches in your life:

1. Find your community. Ask for help and support from people who have experienced what you are experiencing. Going through fertility challenges? Don't seek advice from your friend Fertile Myrtle, who had four babies already. Go find a fertility-challenged support group with people that are experiencing the same challenges you are. Those people, who have walked in your shoes, will have better, comforting words for you than those who haven't. They can sit with you in the muck and have empathy for you versus just telling you how to fix your problems. Sounds pretty obvious, but think about who you go to for support. Are they people who have gone through similar challenges? When you're in the thick of a challenge, it's important to have seasoned pros in your corner.

After years of hip pain and finally an MRI, a surgeon told me that I would inevitably need a hip replacement. I cried in his office. I was forty years old at the time, which is considered very young for that kind of surgery. Unless, of course, there's nothing left to do except just live with the pain. Friends would give me advice to either wait as long as I could, or just get it over with, but they had no clue or experience with my particular situation. So, I set out to find people who did. I found a private Facebook group of young people who have had hip-replacement surgeries. They call themselves "hipsters," and they ask and answer questions about pain management, pre- and post-op protocols, and surgery styles, and share their stories of challenges and success. Reading their posts makes me realize that there are people all around the globe who can be there to catch my fall and help me back up with moral support when it's my turn.

2. Share your story. Feelings of guilt and shame usually go hand in hand with failure. Many people will shove these feelings deep down inside, never to see the light of day. However, most times these feelings will rear their ugly head in self-destructive behaviors, like numbing with food, alcohol, or drugs, or in destructive patterns in relationships, or in not claiming your worth in your professional life. Sharing your story helps release the pent-up shame and guilt in a healthy way.

Business failures can be shared with colleagues for them to learn from. Relationship failures can be shared with friends going through similar challenges. Diseases, disabilities, and health challenges that are not obvious to the outside world can be shared instead of hiding them in shame. Sharing challenges and failures makes you more relatable as a person, and therefore allows you to have deeper connectedness in relationships. It also helps make topics like miscarriage, abortion, divorce, death, or mental illness less taboo. And can we PLEASE make these topics, and others, less taboo?

Not everyone wants to share their most embarrassing failure or private challenge on Instagram for the world to hear, and that's more than okay. Sharing it with a few friends or family members can open up some room to heal. And if that's even too close for comfort, sharing it with a therapist or trained counselor is just as helpful. Keeping it bottled up inside is not helpful.

3. Adopt a "happy failure" mindset. Sara Blakely, founder of Spanx, says her father would ask her every night at dinner what she had failed at that day in school. If she didn't fail at something, he would actually be disappointed. Sound weird? Her dad doubled down on ensuring his kids knew that you have to fail at things in order to succeed. You have to put yourself out there and take risks in order to live a full, kick-ass life. Adopting that mindset allows failures to become part of the journey to success instead of derailing the journey altogether.

Most people didn't have that style of parenting. But it's not too late to give yourself that gift instead. Give yourself permission to fail, knowing that you must in order to do great things. You can give yourself permission to collect many nos in order to get a yes. Whether you apply that mindset to dating or sales, it sets you up for resilience, which is necessary to achieve big wins.

4. Own your mistakes. If you mess up big time, it can really eff with your confidence. If there is anything you need to apologize for or own, if there is anyone you have hurt in the process, take some time to deal with it. Write an apology e-mail to someone you hurt or the employees you had to fire due to your mistakes. You don't have to send the letter, but be sure to write it.

Maybe you need to apologize to yourself? Are you the one who cheated in your relationship? Did you take a giant risk with money that wasn't yours and lose? Did you betray a friend's trust? Failing yourself and your own values can sometimes feel worse than the hurt you've caused another. If you're holding yourself in a prison of self-hatred for what you've done, in order to move on, write yourself that letter and read it over and over until you begin to believe it.

OYH Exercise: Rolling with the Punches

1. Clear some space on the floor. Lay down a yoga mat, if you have one, or a soft blanket on the floor. If you don't have either and your floors are really hard, you can try this exercise on your bed.

2. Sit on the floor or bed with your knees bent, and wrap your arms around them. Tuck yourself into a tiny ball by dropping your chin to your chest and rounding your spine.

3. Now let yourself roll backward and then forward to your starting position.

4. Imagine a challenge you're dealing with that's pushing you back and, no matter what, the momentum you have allows you to roll right back up to a seat again. If you have the strength and the practice, try getting your feet underneath you and standing up at the finish.

The Ultimate Comeback

Pivoting and rolling are awesome. Then there's the next level kinda comebacks. This happens when someone creates something off-the-charts amazing and beautiful out of something tragic and traumatic. This is the chin-dropping kind of magic that leaves people completely awestruck. This is what I call the ultimate comeback.

These kinds of comebacks are rare because they usually come from really horrific circumstances where pivoting and even rolling may not be enough. Sometimes your dreams are shattered and torn into a million little pieces. Or something or someone has been taken away from you either through death or divorce, and there's no chance of it or them coming back. The only option left is to re-create your life into something completely new and awe inspiring.

Extraordinary people usually have great comeback stories. Most business moguls have failed terribly at business and went on to make millions. Tons of celebrities have turned their tragic moments into motivation to bring their talents to the world. Then there are tons of us regular people, with untold stories of tragedy and loss, and we too have turned our lives around. It doesn't usually happen overnight. It can take years, even decades to turn those scars into success. Here are some examples to use as inspiration:

- My friend Laurenne lost her dad to suicide when she was sixteen years old. Now, at age forty, she's become a grief counselor to help others walk through the grieving process.

- Malala Yousafzai was shot in the head by a member of the Taliban for going to school as a girl. She won the Nobel Peace Prize for her activism around girls' access to education.

- Adrianne Haslet lost part of her leg to a bomb during the Boston Marathon. She adapted to a prosthetic and went on to achieve her dream of becoming a ballroom dancer and motivational speaker.

In 2015, I received an e-mail from a television producer who wanted me to audition for a new reality TV show in production. I jumped at the chance. The producer was interested in my approach to weight loss and thought I would be a good fit for the show, but I wouldn't know if I would actually get a spot on the show until after it started production.

The premise of the show was that each weight-loss contestant had their own weight-loss coach. Each coach had their own plan of fitness and nutrition to help their client lose the most weight. Each client could fire their coach one time only. I was the backup coach who would replace a coach once they were fired. Essentially, I was on call.

Finally, the call came from the producer that I was to pack up and get on a plane to Atlanta to film for the next six weeks, and I had to leave in two days. I was actually going to be on a reality TV show on a major network. Move over, Jillian Michaels. This was the big break that I had been waiting for my entire career.

I flew to Atlanta on my birthday and started working with my client immediately. My client, Taj, and I got along fine enough. There were plenty of differences in our personalities, but I was 100 percent committed to getting her to the finish line. We changed up her diet to a pescatarian and wheat-free meal plan, and I was training her in martial arts.

The other contestants got along with their coaches really well. There was Dawn and Jasmine whose philosophy was that weight loss can be joyful, and you can never have too much glitter. There was Jay and Jeff who wound up getting matching tattoos. Abel and Kurt had their own bromance going on. And even Rob and Latasha enjoyed each other's company so much that they went for pedicures together. Everyone was on board with their coach's plan, and everyone was losing weight. But on the next team challenge (running around a track), Taj just up and quit. That began the downfall of our coach/client relationship.

I did my best in the next few weeks to move past our personal differences and poured my energy into making sure my client felt supported and was on her way to possibly winning this show. But then it all blew up. In the second-to-last episode, I had planned to test Taj for her yellow belt in martial arts. I had a belt and uniform flown in from the dojo in NYC where I had trained and thought that I had prepared my student both mentally and physically for the challenge to move from white belt to yellow belt. I was wrong.

Somewhere toward the very end of the test, I could see Taj was starting to lose it. She was struggling to finish the push-ups and planks I saved for the end. I encouraged her to finish the fight. She began to shut down. Her face looked annoyed as I congratulated her for finishing up strong. I asked her what had happened, and all she said on repeat was, "I'm tired." Right, so that's what happens when you push yourself to the limits. Her attitude sparked a fuse in me, and I lost my shit on camera. The weeks of her negative attitude leading up to this moment had bubbled up inside me, and I couldn't hold back. I raised my voice, I dropped the F-bomb on national TV, and I told her that I was done. That we were done.

So the next day when we were filming the weigh-in with the rest of the group, Taj quit the show and, therefore, I was technically fired from the show. I failed. Big time. Not only did my client not win the competition (Dawn and Jasmine did), I didn't even get my client to the finish line. Not only would I not achieve Jillian Michaels status, I'd probably be the laughingstock of the fitness industry. I was seriously concerned my career would be over.

I couldn't have been more wrong. ABC-TV premiered its newest weight-loss reality show, *My Diet Is Better Than Yours,* in January 2016. The night that dreadful episode was airing, I was cringing on my couch and embracing the suck. I was ready for public humiliation to begin. But a really funny thing happened. Instead of people ridiculing me, I started to hear from people all over the country through social media. They were cheering me on. They appreciated my effort in trying to change the conversation around weight loss. At the end of the day, it's not just about calories in versus calories out. Mindset is the most important tool that needs to be strengthened as you journey to a more fit body.

I rolled with the punches. Then, I got back on my feet, and I wound up making an ultimate comeback by pursuing a career in public speaking. Something that I had been wanting to do for the past decade but never had the grit to go after. Now, I had failed publicly on national TV and I didn't die! Why NOT put myself out there and chase my dreams? To date, I've spoken to tens of thousands of women at colleges, conferences, and corporations on the many ways to empower oneself. I'm living my dreams and doing my best to inspire other women to do the same. Maybe a little public humiliation and failure were exactly what I needed? Ya think?

OYH Exercise: The Comeback

1. Sit on the floor and be as dramatic as you'd like to be. You can pretend the fiercest opponent has just knocked you down.

2. Shake it off and stand back up in a victorious position; tilt your chin up high and fix your eyes on your opponent.

3. Say out loud: "I GOT THIS!"

How to Experience an Ultimate Comeback

After practicing the Comeback on your mat, use that "I got this!" feeling as you make your way through the following five-step process for designing your own comebacks in life.

1. Give yourself grace. After a life-altering event, give yourself time and space to grieve the losses you may have suffered. Whether those losses are dreams, relationships, money, or people, they are still losses that cause feelings of grief. Feel the feelings for as long as you need to process them before moving on.

Remember that burying feelings is never good for the long run. You must let them be expressed in order to move them through your body. Trauma, drama, and heartache can get stuck and take years or even a lifetime to move on from if you don't actively work on them.

2. Reimagine. Maybe your business has completely failed and there is no turning it around. Reimagine a completely new career path for yourself. Maybe you've experienced a divorce or the death of a loved one. There is no option to pivot or roll when that relationship no longer exists, but you can reimagine what your life can be like without the person. This step takes some creativity and out-of-the-box thinking, so give yourself plenty of room to imagine a new, beautiful scenario.

3. Re-create. Map out a plan for your comeback. It may include going back to school or learning a new skill. It may involve researching new ways of doing things. Once you have mapped out your plan, hang it somewhere where you will see it every day.

Having a map for your comeback will help steer you in the right direction. As you navigate the newest version of your life, keep that map as your guiding star. Taking small, consistent actions toward your new vision signals your spirit to stay motivated and committed to your goals.

4. Ignore the naysayers. You will have to ignore the haters in order to experience an ultimate comeback. Small people will do their best to talk you out of re-creating yourself and try to keep you playing small.

5. Set your plan in motion. You have your plan, now it's time to act on it. Get the help you need and some accountability to make it happen.

My favorite quote from Mike Dooley, the creator of *Notes from the Universe,* states, "Do the best you can with what you have from where you're at." Meaning, even small, consistent steps each day toward your dream eventually lead to badass results.

Remember that nobody does life alone. The most successful, happy people have help. I've had many types of coaches throughout my adult life. My martial arts instructors taught me skills that range from getting out of chokeholds to leadership principles. I have a mindset coach who helps me through crises or a general leveling up of my game. I've hired multiple business coaches to help me expand my business. Each one would help move me from one level to the next. All of them were equally important to my progress, and I never regret any money that I've invested in my personal and professional growth. What type of support can you use as you make your ultimate comeback?

Does your ultimate comeback include:

- A financial makeover? Find a financial coach to help you make a debt repayment plan, or a fiduciary, to help guide you in setting up your investments.

- A career makeover? Find a business or career coach who can help guide you in building your résumé and networking to find your next career move.

- A new intimate relationship? Find a dating coach (yes, they exist).

- A reboot to your health? Find private fitness groups on Facebook, online trainers or coaches, or running groups. Search for local or online healthy cooking classes if you need help with your nutrition.

- A comeback from the death of a loved one? Find a grief counselor or therapist to help walk you through the darkness.

Don't let money be the only obstacle stopping you from getting help. There are plenty of free services, information, and accountability groups that you can find either locally or online to help you reach your goals.

Belt Test: Yellow to Orange (#badassbelttest)

PREPARE FOR YOUR TEST

1. You'll prepare for every belt test in the same way that you did for your white belt test. Clear some dedicated space in the room. If you wish, make your belt test feel sacred by adding any special scents, sounds, or clothes to mark the occasion.

2. Now step onto your "mat" and give yourself a deep bow of love and respect.

START YOUR TEST

It's time to give yourself proof that you have mastered the art of bouncing back.

1. Take out your journal and favorite pen. Begin to remember times in your life when you've been knocked down. You will probably find some on your Greatest (S)hits List.

2. For each entry, think about how you recovered from that knockout and answer the following prompts:
   • Did you pivot?
   • Did you practice bouncing back?
   • Did you make an ultimate comeback?

- Think of an avatar or metaphor of who you became through that transformation. A ninja? A phoenix? A lion?

- What are the traits of that avatar or metaphor? For example: A lion is fierce and, when messed with, will roar for the entire world to hear.

3. Give yourself props for handling your past challenges and perceived failures. Write a few sentences to congratulate yourself for getting back up after each knockout. Write to yourself as enthusiastically as you would speak to your best friend. Read this out loud to yourself and let those feelings of badassery sink in.

You did it! You completed your belt test. You proved to yourself that you have the ability to get back up after a knockout and you will be able to do it time and time again. You are now an orange belt. 🏮

CHAPTER THREE

Orange Belt: Block the BS

A friend once told me a story about when she was a med student doing hospital rotations, and an orthopedic surgeon asked her to assist him with a knee replacement. She felt honored to be chosen until, in the middle of the surgery, he started spraying her with water. "Wet T-shirt contest!" he shouted as everyone laughed. "Everyone" being the three male students observing the procedure, the male anesthesiologist, and the male surgical tech. The only person not laughing was the circulating nurse who was the only other woman in the room. "We made eye contact and then she kept doing her job as if she'd seen this all before, and it's just the way it is," my friend described. Meanwhile, she felt she had to "swallow the tears, suck it up, and play along."

This type of scenario plays out in countless ways that we've all experienced—those moments where we're left dumbfounded, humiliated, or pissed off by the insensitive, unkind, and unfair actions of others.

- We're catcalled on the street so often that we've become numb to it.

- Our bodies have been objectified in the media as well as in real life when people comment on our shape, size, or weight.

- Our bodies have been touched without consent time and time again.

- We've been mansplained or outright dismissed by others.

- Our ideas have been hijacked and repackaged at work.

- We've been passed over for positions, promotions, and projects that were given to male counterparts simply because they were male.

And we know we're not alone in these experiences. According to a recent online survey conducted by a nonprofit called Stop Street Harassment, 81 percent of women have experienced some form of sexual harassment. According to the World Health Organization, one in three women globally will be a victim of sexual violence.

It's heavy. These instances chip away at our confidence and our power, both individually and collectively as women. They rob us of our peace and distract us from our purpose. We can no longer afford this. This world needs us to preserve our innate power and block all the many different kinds of BS from getting in our way. This chapter will provide tools to block the negativity and help you to stop taking shit from others.

What It Means to Be an Orange Belt

Orange belts in martial arts focus on learning how to block the punches and kicks that come their way. If they don't learn how to block all the incoming assaults, they're going to get punched in the face or kicked in the gut and wind up in some serious pain. So they practice their blocks over and over again, like the Karate Kid. Wax on, wax off. Paint the fence. That way, when they're faced with a side kick coming in hot, their body automatically knows which block to use and executes with precision.

As an orange belt, you'll learn how to protect yourself by blocking negative bullshit. During my self-defense seminars I teach women they have two options if someone is following them on the street: create distance from that person or confront them with your boundaries. In other areas of life, I offer women the same options—whether faced with a verbal assault, a condescending comment, a mansplainer, or someone who is trying to take advantage of them.

We are powerful and precious, and therefore we need to protect our spirits. Luckily, we're born with primal instincts similar to animals in the wild. Animals make decisions based on their core instinct for survival. Humans, on the other hand, are the only animals that second-guess and even ignore those instincts at times. Somewhere along the way, women especially are conditioned out of following their instincts. We'd rather be polite than assert ourselves. We worry about hurting a person's feelings before protecting our own. Going forward, we'll know how to unleash those primal instincts to our advantage and stand up for ourselves when necessary, no matter what anyone thinks.

It may take some practice to get used to, especially if you've spent your whole life accommodating others and making them feel comfortable at your own expense. But I can promise you that the more you use the following techniques, the more powerful you'll feel, which will lead to more peace within. When you have more peace within, you have more space for a purpose-filled life.

If you haven't been able to block the BS in your life in the past, it's okay. There are many reasons why people choose not to block or wish they chose a better way to deal with the BS. When people throw manipulative language, negative comments, or verbal assaults at us, they can activate our fight-or-flight response. Our brains get hijacked, our bodies release stress hormones, and we may have an intense desire to fight, flee the situation, or freeze and shut down altogether.

When we're relaxed, our body is better able to recover from stressful situations, and our brains are able to tap into logical thinking and creativity. It's a much more resourceful state to be in when figuring out how to respond to a nonphysical attack like a rude or misogynistic comment. Taking a beat to regain your composure is going to give you a chance to intentionally choose the response that will help you gain power in the situation. The next time you're in a super-stressful state that feels like you are under attack, check in with your body. You'll probably feel a tightness in your chest along with shallow and quick breathing patterns. Just notice it at first. Then gradually start to slow down your breathing, and allow it to become deeper and deeper. Notice if that frees up space to then channel the appropriate response you want.

OYH Exercise: Breathwork

Deep belly breathing can help you reset your nervous system and allow you to enter a more relaxed and resourceful state. Let's practice now so we can build the habit of taking a deep breath or five to stay calm and focused in the face of adversity.

1. Inhale through your nose and fill up your belly with air.
2. Hold for a few seconds at the top of the breath and then slowly exhale.
3. Start by practicing that for a few rounds and check in to see how you feel.

The more you practice the longer you can increase the inhale, the hold, and the exhale. Try starting with a pattern of:

- Inhale for 2 counts. Hold for 2 counts. Exhale for 2 counts. Do this for at least 4 cycles.

The next time you find yourself in a stressful state try increasing the pattern to:

- Inhale for 3 counts. Hold for 3 counts. Exhale for 3 counts. Do this for at least 6 cycles.

And then the next time try:

- Inhale for 4 counts. Hold for 4 counts. Exhale for 4 counts. Do this for up to 10 cycles.

And so on, until you feel it working for you. This is called the 4x4x4 method.

During a dangerous and physically violent attack, you probably won't have time to use this full technique. But even remembering that it's there for you can help you make better decisions. You may be able to sneak in a deep breath or two before choosing to run, hide, or fight back. You may be able to remind yourself that your fear response is taking over. You may even be able to choose a better way to act in the moment. Don't blame yourself for how you think you should have acted in the past. Take your power back now by preparing for how you will act if faced with a similar situation in the future. Move on with power and intention.

For the rest of this chapter, we'll deal mostly with verbal attacks, insults, and attitudes. Things most of us face in our daily lives, which doesn't necessarily make them less difficult to handle.

Real-life examples of effed-up comments my clients and friends have been on the receiving end of:

- As Sally and her husband interviewed a potential investment advisor, Sally's husband said, "Explain it so that Sally can understand."
- Lani was on a date and her Prince Charming said, "Have you thought about getting your boobs done?" She replied in shock, "Excuse me?" He continued, "Well if you lost some weight and had better proportions, you'd be beautiful!"
- Kate was told by her boss that she was "too fat to work in fashion."
- Erin had a boss say to her, "You should be paying me for all that you're learning from us" after asking for the raise she was promised during a glowing review.
- Nubia was told by a white man, "You only got that job because you're black."
- Kelly's boss handed her, "You're not cool enough for this role. We're looking for someone a little . . . cooler."

Options for Blocking the Bullshit

In any situation with a person where you feel degraded, weak, vulnerable, or manipulated, ask yourself:

1. Can I create distance from this person or situation?

2. Do I need to set boundaries for this situation?

3. Which type of boundary setting feels right for this person or situation?

- Redirection (soft block)
- Hard line (hard block)

The answer to these questions will lead you to one or more of the following tactics.

"The ultimate aim of martial arts is not having to use them."
—**Miyamoto Musashi,** sixteenth-century Japanese samurai, author, and artist

Creating Distance

In martial arts, the goal is always not to fight. It may seem counterintuitive, but physical self-defense is always the last resort. True martial artists try to avoid unnecessary conflict and save their energy for fighting for causes they truly believe in. They will walk away from a bar fight created from ego but walk into a fight to stick up for their deserved promotion, their loved ones, or social justice.

Creating distance from the fight that is unworthy of us is the simplest way to block bullshit, and it might look like any of these examples:

- You're being catcalled on the street. It's late and there are no other people around. Stores are closed, and it's just you and the harasser. In this scenario, when your safety may be at stake, the safest choice may be to ignore and move away as quickly as possible.

- You're at a bar, waiting on your girlfriends. The guy next to you is hitting on you, and you're not into it. Your comfort level for confrontation is low at the moment, so grabbing a seat at the other end of the bar would be a good option to create distance and avoid a potential confrontation.

- You've posted on your favorite social media account, and a troll comments by calling you names. Ignoring the troll lets you avoid stooping to their level and feeding their energy. Sometimes rising above and ignoring the bullshit are the best options.

These examples are with people you most likely don't know or don't care about. Creating distance can be a much more difficult option if the person you are detaching from is a partner, friend, colleague, or family member. It may mean changing the relationship dynamic or even leaving the relationship altogether.

Every situation and every relationship is unique and therefore should not be subject to some generic rule book. You have to feel things out. Will detaching from this relationship serve you for your greater good? Will it help you feel powerful, even though it may hurt initially? Or does creating space from a person simply mean being less available to them? That can be more easily done by not answering their texts or phone calls instantly. Or that could mean getting out of town for a couple of days to spend some time by yourself and not being available for a limited amount of time. Creating space needs to serve you. It should provide time for you to regain your composure and powerfully choose how you want to proceed (perhaps with some of the blocks coming up). Examples of this can look like:

- Your boss said something really nasty to you when you weren't able to meet her needs. You take a beat by taking a day off in the immediate future to fill your cup and decide how you want to be treated by her going forward.

- A relative keeps pressing you about when you're going to have kids, and you keep your distance for a few weeks until they get the hint.

- Your partner says something really hurtful to you and you decide to take the weekend to hang out with your girlfriends instead of with him or her.

It doesn't have to mean leaving the relationship altogether, but sometimes that's an option as well.

OYH Exercise: Creating Distance

Embodying the ability to create distance from a negative person or comment will help you when the time comes to mentally create some much-needed space.

1. Stand with soft knees and fists held up by your face like a boxer.

2. Envision a verbal assault or someone's negative energy coming your way.

3. Step far out to the left with your left foot.

4. Slide your right foot to meet your left.

5. Do the same with your right foot beginning and left following.

6. Repeat ten times. Slide away. Shake it off. No negativity will stick to you.

Setting Boundaries

Setting boundaries is a lot easier when you're clear about what you want in relationships with people and how you want to be treated. Too many times I see women giving away their power without a second thought about what they really want. I've been there too. When I was in my teens and twenties, I went along with sexual encounters I wasn't really into just because the guy wanted it. I've let a client speak to me in a condescending way because I thought if I spoke up, I would lose her as a client. I know women who let their partners verbally abuse them after a few drinks, and they tolerate it even though they logically know it's abusive behavior. Why do we allow ourselves to be walked all over by certain people? It's probably because we haven't clearly defined how we want to feel in relationships and when we need to set boundaries.

Obviously, we assume that inappropriate, rude, or abusive behavior should not be tolerated by anyone. But there are going to be creeps and energy vampires out there who have boundary blinders on or are just downright predatory jerks. What next? Do we lay down and become doormats? Do we rise up forcibly and block? Do we tolerate it for a bit and then change the dynamic of the relationship? I wish I could say it was easy to just block all the bullshit that comes your way the second it comes. But we all know from experience that situations are much more nuanced than that.

During that unhealthy relationship I mentioned in the first chapter, I let a LOT of things slide. Conversations that didn't make sense. Gaslighting. You name it. I gave into the power dynamic of him having perceived power over me (he was much older than me and an authority figure), and after a while I stopped asking questions and stopped speaking up. I tolerated the bullshit.

After the breakup, I got clear that I valued trust, respect, open communication, and honesty. Therefore, in any type of relationship, I would get into going forward, personally and professionally, if those values were challenged, I would need to set boundaries. I would no longer tolerate feeling disrespected, or not having trust, open communication, or honesty present.

If you look back to times in your life when people have thrown some nasty crap your way, you'll be able to find your values being defaced or ignored. You'll be able to find the instances where your power has been depleted. And you'll be able to find the times when you let the shit stick to you, because you tolerated it for way too long.

Exercise: Your Hell Yes List

It's time to get clear on how you want to feel in your personal and professional relationships and what you will no longer tolerate so it will be clear when you need to set boundaries and choose which kind are best for your situation going forward. Grab a journal and a pen.

1. Write down three categories of relationships: romantic partners, personal relationships, and professional relationships, or just focus on the one area that you'd like. At the very least, choose the one where you feel the most lack of power.

2. Ask yourself how you want to feel in those types of relationships.

3. Write down all the feelings that come to mind that may or may not include feeling loved, emotionally safe, physically safe, financially safe, respected, appreciated, adventurous, equal, passionate, trusted, supported, open, and anything else that feels important to you.

4. Circle the top five feelings that you really want to feel in your relationships, and let's start with those.

5. Write those five feelings down at the top of a clean page. These are your Hell Yes feelings. These feelings will become your North Star, guiding you and pulling you toward people, places, and things that evoke these feelings. When these feelings are present in a situation or in a relationship, you'll feel like your needs are getting met, and your values are not being challenged.

6. Now check in with a person who falls into one of your three categories. For example, if you have a boss, check to see if your boss makes you feel the way you want to feel in a professional relationship. If that's a Hell Yes, wonderful. You most likely feel supported and in a good place. If not, move on to your Hell No List to see if there are boundaries that need to be set to help you take your power back.

Exercise: Your Hell No List

Your Hell No List is the opposite of your Hell Yes List. This list will help you get really clear on which situations and relationships in your life are going to need some serious boundary setting.

1. Take your top five Hell Yes feelings and find their exact opposite. For example, feeling loved would become feeling unloved. Feeling emotionally safe would become feeling emotionally unsafe.

2. Write those five feelings down and label them your Hell No List. These feelings become your red flag feelings. Anytime you feel these feelings, consider it a warning and a time to check in with yourself to see how the following blocking

strategies may help you protect and preserve your peace, power, and happiness.

3. Go a step farther. Think of what actions, traits, or behaviors from other people make you feel this way. Said another way, what will you absolutely NOT tolerate from another person or situation? This step can get you crystal clear on what to look out for and put a stop to before it happens or even in the moment. You can use the following prompts to help guide you:

- What are the ways people have treated you in the past that make your blood boil?
- What are you still tolerating that is slowly zapping your peace and power?

For example, if the Hell No feeling is disrespect, then belittling your beliefs or putting yourself down in front of your colleagues would be actions that need to be blocked.

If the Hell No feeling is inequality in a partnered relationship, then being responsible for all the housework while you both hold down full-time jobs is a situation that needs some blocking.

If the Hell No feeling in a friendship is inauthenticity, then having a friend who is fake and shallow with you is a relationship that could use some distance or boundary setting.

Real-Time Blocking Techniques

You can know your boundaries in relationships and still find yourself in situations where you need tools to combat the BS in real time because you can't, or just aren't willing to, walk away. This is when it pays to have as many blocks in your arsenal to use depending on the situation.

Martial arts is the umbrella term for many styles of self-defense. Some arts, like karate or boxing, use hard techniques, meaning they meet force with an equal and opposing force. In softer styles of martial arts, like kung fu or aikido, the defender redirects the attacker's force against him or her, away from the defender, instead of meeting the attack with a direct forceful block.

In real life, on the streets or in the boardroom, we have similar options: soft blocks or hard blocks against people's BS.

Soft Blocks

A soft block redirects the bullshit that someone just sent your way. It can be visualized kind of like a dance. Utilizing the momentum of your opponent's attack, you can redirect it either out into space or in a circular motion right back at them. This can be done in different ways and is more effective than hard blocks in many situations. Here are five different soft blocks you can use depending on your unique situation.

1. The deflection

To deflect is to cause something to change direction by interposing something else. In this case, a deflection can be used to change the course of a conversation that is heading in a direction that you don't want to go to or when a comment is made that you would rather not address.

Insults and put-downs that sting but don't threaten can be handled this way. Your mother-in-law comments on your cooking in a not-so-obvious but definitely negative way in front of your husband's entire family. You know that keeping the peace may be your best option in the long run or that this particular instance isn't the right time to confront her. If so, changing the subject to your accomplishments at work can be a great way to take the focus off your meatballs. Perhaps later, when you two are having a private moment, you can use a different technique (like #3) to let her know how her comments make you feel.

2. The clarification

Clarifying the intent behind someone's comment allows you to get back in the driver's seat when a conversation goes sideways. It's a softer way of handling things like backhanded compliments or complisults: the merger of an insult and a compliment. These things can be given intentionally or unintentionally, and it's best to find out which so you know what kind of person you're dealing with and how to handle them in the future. If the complisult was given unintentionally, then you can clear up the communication and move on. Perhaps the giver of the complisult may be more aware of their words in the future. If the person's words were intentional, then you may be dealing with someone who can't give compliments freely or may be trying to "keep you in your place." If that's the case, it may be time to take a look at your relationship with the person and see if creating some distance from them is an option!

You can use this block by simply being direct and asking the person for clarification on their meaning and intent. In the past you may have kept quiet and left the conversation while scratching your head and wondering. Now you'll know!

Examples:
- You have such a pretty face. If you'd lose some weight, you'd be a stunner!

Clarification: Are you saying I'm not a stunner now and that you think my weight is what stops me from being a stunner?

- Wow. That is some dress. Is that what you're wearing?
  Clarification: Why yes, I am wearing this dress. Are you trying to say that you think I shouldn't wear this for some reason?

- You look really pretty with makeup on.
  Clarification: Are you saying that you think I am not pretty without makeup?

- You look great, for your age.
  Clarification: Why do you need to clarify that I look great *for my age?*

- Nice job on that presentation. I was surprised you did so well.
  Clarification: Oh really? Why would you be surprised that I nailed a presentation?

3. Tell them how it lands

This technique is great for people who are in touch with their emotions. When someone insults you, your work, your body, etc., in the moment you know it doesn't feel good. Identify the feeling and then ask the affronter, "Your comment made me feel {fill in the blank}. Was that your intention?"

Many times, the insulter is not even aware of the impact of their words. Think of this technique as helping someone else become more aware of their speech and how it affects others. This is a good technique for friends and family members who may not understand your lifestyle choices and may say things that hurt your feelings like, "Isn't it about time you get married?" or "When are you going to have kids? You won't be young forever." Letting these people know how their words make you feel in the moment is a way to stand in your power without letting their opinions take you down. And who knows, it may even open up some room for a conversation!

4. Follow up with a question

An incisive question is a great way to hold people accountable for their actions. Hold their gaze until they answer the question to punctuate your stance and create an agreement for the future.

Examples:

- "Greg, do you think it's appropriate to comment on my body, ever, but especially at work?" Hold stare. Watch him flounder. Wait for an answer. Reply with, "Don't do it again."

- "Chelsea, why are you questioning the way I handled the customer who was being rude to me? Do you have a better suggestion of how I should have handled it?"

- "{Boss's name}, your tone of voice sounds very intense and stern. Is there a reason why you're speaking to me in that way?"

- "Honey, I understand you had a bad day at work. Is that a reason to take it out on me?"

5. The deadly stare

People hate awkward silence. If you were just handed an insult or negative comment, stare at the offender with an icy gaze and hold it for five long, awkward seconds until the person squirms.

OYH Exercise: Soft Block

Let's do a quick exercise to help you internalize what soft blocking feels like.

1. Stand up and soften your knees.

2. Take a few long, deep breaths. In through the nose, out through the mouth. Fill up the belly on the inhale, and let it go on the exhale. Feel the ground supporting you.

3. Now picture a wad of crap coming your way. With open hands, you will reach toward the crap, blend with its force coming toward you, and then in a circular motion redirect it toward the crap thrower.

4. Repeat these circular motions ten times and keep picturing the crap heading toward them or out into space.

5. Say out loud five times, "I will not be moved by your bullshit. I am powerful. I am peaceful. I am on purpose."

Hard Blocks

A hard block is the more confrontational option to use when you're feeling attacked, dismissed, or taken advantage of. When the attack comes at you, confront your attacker head-on with an equal or greater amount of force. You can use your voice, your body, or a combination of the two. What follows are five hard block options to choose from, depending on the situation and what feels right to you.

1. Shut it down

Do you ever find yourself explaining, ad nauseam, why you're saying no to some crap you don't want in your life? No. Nope. Never. All one-word sentences that are complete as they are.

Don't want to go with the guy at the bar who keeps asking you to join him for just one more drink? Nope! Don't want to sleep with someone after making out? No. Don't feel like taking the client out to dinner who has made a comment about your ass? Never. Don't want to serve the table of men who are getting drunker and lewder by the minute? Hell no.

We often feel like we need to explain to people why something doesn't feel right or why we're turning down an unwanted advance. Here's your reminder that you are not obligated to do so. A firm "no" is not up for discussion. In a best-case scenario, exit after your firm no. If someone doesn't respect your no, then you may have to advance to one of the next techniques.

If the block doesn't warrant a no, then a direct opposing response would also be an option here. "Never speak to me that way again" is a hard NO that's more specific to the situation. "I'm not having this discussion/argument with you." "Never say that to me again." Shut it down with a direct sentence with no explanation necessary.

2. Stand your ground

We often use the term "stand your ground" in a figurative way, to describe a refusal to change your opinion or give in to an argument. I want you to get literal with this statement. Stand in a powerful position. If you were seated at the time of verbal assault, stand up. Feel strong in your body. Some men use their stature to intimidate; so can you. Pull your shoulders back, keep your head held high, take your deep breath, and then deliver your hard block whether that is a firm no or another technique that follows.

3. Use strong, shocking language

"Back the FUCK up! I've had it with your misogynistic BULL-SHIT. How dare you FUCKING belittle me in front of my friends! Never FUCKING speak to me in that tone again you piece of SHIT. Get your FUCKING hands off me!"

If reading those sentences makes you feel uncomfortable, then GOOD! That's what they are there to do. Most people who take on predatory behavior are not expecting you to fight back, let alone use harsh language. The shock factor will sometimes be enough for a predator, whether that is a stranger or your manager, to back off. If foul language is something you're known to use on the regular, then this shock factor may not be as effective as for someone who rarely curses. I suggest using your foul fucking language with discernment and intention.

4. Threaten with authority

This technique is especially useful when you find yourself being harassed in a professional setting or a setting where you don't feel comfortable enough to tell someone off. Perhaps your boss or a colleague makes an unwanted advance; threatening to talk to human resources or your colleague's boss can be a way to bring in authority for accountability. Threatening to call the police is another example of this technique and should be reserved for a crime or attempted crime.

There are plenty of reasons why some women won't use this block, especially in a work environment. Often, it's because they fear they may lose their job or make the situation worse. That is completely understandable. You have to do what you think is right for your particular situation.

For women who don't work in corporate America and don't have a human resources professional to report to, this technique can be even trickier. If you work in a restaurant and the chef harasses you, can you report the incident to the manager or owner? They may not care or even believe you. What if the harasser is the manager or owner? If you work for yourself and a client harasses you, can you report the behavior to their senior? You may not want to for fear of losing the client. Even in these very tricky situations, you may want to throw in that you've told someone else about the bad behavior, even if it's your girlfriend. Put it all in writing so you have a record of the incident for future reference. Send an e-mail to your friend describing the incident with the where, what, when, and who. Creeps want to manipulate you in private. They don't want anyone else to know about it, and they won't want anyone else advising you on how to handle the situation.

*Please note: If your safety is ever in danger, get the help of a professional as soon as possible.

5. Use your body as a weapon

When things get really heated, sometimes you need to throw your body into the mix to deliver a full body block. Many of us were never taught to use our body as a weapon or that it's strong and powerful enough to do so in the first place. Yet time and time again, I hear stories of women who have fought back against attempted assaults even with no prior training. I believe there's something primal in all of us that allows us to tap into our inner protector and use our body as a weapon if and when we need to. Over centuries, that trigger may have been trained out of us, but the ability is still there.

Let's get primal: Think of something you want more than anything right now. A million dollars? An adorable rescue puppy? A pizza with extra cheese? Imagine someone offering that thing to you with no strings attached and you giving a full-body YES as you accept it. Feel how your body opens up and energetically expresses this wish being answered.

Now picture someone taking away that precious gift from you. Just trying to snatch it from your grasp even though it is rightfully yours. Do you puff up your chest and say no with your eyes? Do you put your hand out to stop them? Do you point your fingers while doing it? Do you widen your stance and use your voice in a deep, powerful yell? Do you grab the person's hand and squeeze it with as much force as you can muster? Or do you about-face and walk away from the situation entirely? If you can use that force to protect money, a puppy, or some pizza, you can find that power to protect your body and yourself by delivering a full-body NO.

In many instances, we may have to use a combination of more than one technique. I once trained a client in a luxury Beverly Hills hotel for a month. He was a slender guy from the Middle East who refused to work out in the hotel gym. So, like any logical billionaire would do, he bought a treadmill and used one of the hotel rooms in the entire wing he had rented as his own personal gym. The gig was good money for me for little effort. I'd go to his hotel room for an hour and make him walk on the treadmill, occasionally pushing him to do some strengthening exercises. At the end of the hour, I stretched him out for a few minutes and finished!

He scheduled workouts with me Mondays through Fridays for the entire month. On the very last session, on the very last stretch, while I leaned over him holding his leg up, he tried to pull me down on top of him. I stood my ground (technique #2) and brushed it off with some nervous laughter. He finished his stretch, and I let him stand up. I started saying goodbye when he went in for a hug and stuck his face close to mine. "One kiss!" he pleaded. I took both my hands and shoved him hard in his chest, shouting, "No! No kiss!" (techniques #1 and #5). Then I ran out of the room as fast as I could (creating distance) and down the hallway without looking back.

OYH Exercise: Hard Block

Now, let's embody what it feels like to hard block someone's BS by practicing standing your ground and stopping an attack in its tracks.

1. Stand up and stagger your feet.

2. Make your hands into fists and place them near your face so you look like a boxer in her ready stance.

3. Now picture the wad of shit being thrown at you. This time it may have more velocity or volume to it.

4. As it comes to slam you in the face, raise your arm over your head with a 90-degree bent elbow. Picture your forearm meeting the wad with an opposing force equal to or greater than the wad. It stops the wad in its tracks. You hold steady.

5. Do this ten times; five repetitions on each arm. Each time say the word "no" with a deep, unshakable voice.

6. Now stand firm and lock your knees out. Puff out your chest and cross your arms over it. Raise your chin slightly, and stand your ground as shit is thrown your way. You are not moved.

7. Stay in that same stance and now use shocking language. Say out loud, "Back the fuck up!" or any of the phrases you read previously or make up your own! Get comfortable using strong, shocking language.

8. Lastly, go back to that boxer's stance. Visualize the wad coming in hot and throw your hands up and out as if you're pushing the wad away as forcefully as you can. Repeat this motion at least five times. You are powerful. You will not be moved.

How to Decide Which Block to Use

I've gone through many different blocking tactics here, and you may be wondering which to choose and when. There's no absolute right or wrong answer. The tactic used needs to feel right to you and to the moment. My goal for you is for you to never feel stuck again. To know that you have options to block and how to block. To choose which block is right for you and only you. To stop wishing that you could have said something in the past, or should speak up in the future. I want you to stand in your power and make peace with your past decisions and choose how you want to move forward when people are throwing shit your way. Here are a few things to consider when choosing which blocks to use and when.

The Source

Who is the source of the bullshit? As I mentioned before, many women have chosen not to block the BS because of the potential consequences that may be worse than enduring the BS itself. If you can't afford to lose your job, then putting a plan in place to find another one as soon as possible can offer you some peace as you navigate the bullshit, knowing that you're making an effort to remove yourself from the situation. If it's a jerk on the street or in a bar, it may be easier to hard block because you'll never see them again. If it's your neighbor who lives above you, you may choose a softer block because until one of you moves, you're going to keep running into him in the hallway.

Your Confrontation Comfort Zone

Confrontation can be really uncomfortable. Where you come from, your family dynamics, the level of violence in your neighborhood, all contribute to your Confrontation Comfort Zone. If you grew up in a household where screaming at one another was considered normal, then you may have no problem sticking up for yourself in a bold way because you're used to doing it. Or the opposite can be true; because of a more violent household where it felt unsafe to be a kid, you may be completely uncomfortable when anyone begins to raise their voice at all.

Wherever you come from, no matter how you grew up, it's okay to feel how you feel regarding confrontation. Being aware of where you stand can be eye-opening and can give you the ability to choose powerfully about how you would like to deal with confrontation in the future.

Your Bullshit Tolerance

Having some tolerance when it comes to BS can be helpful, because I can pretty much guarantee that, unless you live in a bubble, someone, somewhere is going to throw some shit your way. Your Bullshit Tolerance, the amount of BS you can put up with from someone before you lose your mind, can also stem from childhood. How many insults from the class bully did it take before you broke down and cried or slapped him or her in the face?

In the present moment, your Bullshit Tolerance may also be determined by what else you have going on in your life. If you have an abusive boss, AND you're challenged at home with a sick child or parent, your tolerance for your boss's BS might be quite low. Blocking your boss's BS before it robs you of your peace can be a preemptive approach to staying powerful at work so you can have more patience at home.

Your belief system also matters when it comes to your Bullshit Tolerance. If you're on a date with someone who makes a racist, misogynistic, or homophobic joke and you're someone who believes in equality and speaks up on matters of social justice (or you're just a decent human being), your tolerance will be nonexistent and you'll have no problem serving up a hard block no matter who it is.

Your Safety

Your safety is always priority numero uno. When your safety is on the line, use whatever technique will get you away from the scenario as quickly and safely as possible, and then call for backup. If you ever feel like you're in danger, use your intuition to feel which technique will lead you to safety.

There's Power in Learning

After any encounter like the ones in this chapter, a great way to gain even more power from the situation is to reflect on how you responded. Sometimes we overreact, and sometimes we feel annoyed at ourselves for not acting at all. Whatever the case, use the following steps to help you grow from the experience.

Step one. There's no power in regret. Therefore, in order to generate power from past situations, accept that you did the best you could given the circumstances.

Step two. Own anything that you may have been responsible for. This is NOT about placing blame on the victim. It's about taking responsibility for our lives and our actions, which is really empowering. Was it smart for me to be training a client in his hotel room? Probably not. Could I have put some systems in place to make myself safer, like making sure the front desk knew when I was upstairs in the client's room and asking them to check on me? Sure. Does any of this make it okay for my client to put his hands on me? Absolutely not.

Step three. The reason why we study history is to learn from it and hopefully stop repeating it. Ask yourself if there is anything you have learned from past experience that you can take with you into similar situations in the future. Is there anything you would have done differently? In my particular story, I am clear that if an opportunity like that presented itself again, I would decline. Also, I would have called the client's assistant who originally hired me to let him know what happened. Perhaps then it wouldn't happen to another woman he chooses to hire in the future.

Know the Enemy

Now that you have an arsenal of blocks for all those shit throwers in your life, I'm going to leave you with a reminder of why people sometimes suck. If you're struggling with someone in your life who is trying to take advantage of you, bully you, intimidate you, or demean you, it can help to identify why they're doing it in the first place, so you can stand up for yourself in the best possible way. When someone is rude, passive aggressive, or just a downright bully, there's usually a reason. And guess what? It's usually NOT about you, which can be difficult to accept, but, once you do, it can be absolutely freeing.

> *"If you know the enemy and know yourself, you need not fear the result of a hundred battles."*
> —**Sun Tzu** in *The Art of War*

Five reasons why bullies usually go on the attack include:

1. They are insecure and feel threatened by you. They feel the need to control the situation by putting you down.
2. They are jealous of you! Which makes them feel insecure. See #1.
3. They truly lack understanding of the impact they have on others. They may not believe their actions really matter, which leads to feeling insecure. See #1.
4. They still think that teasing is cool. They want your attention and don't know how to communicate that properly, which makes them feel insecure. See #1.
5. They have a sense of entitlement that leads them to act in obnoxious ways and take what's not rightfully theirs. When you don't give in, it makes them feel insecure. See #1.

So, as you can see, bullies are insecure, immature, and entitled. They come in all shapes and sizes. When we were in elementary school, they were easy to identify: the mean girls who wouldn't let you sit with them in the cafeteria or the boy who pantsed you outside on the playground. But as adults, they might not be so obvious. They might show up as our successful bosses or leaders in our community, and we feel like they somehow deserve our respect. Sometimes they are our friends (or frenemies), members of our family, or our romantic partners.

Whoever they are to you, if they're abusing their perceived power and taking advantage of you or others, then ladies and gentlewomen, we have a problem. From now on, you can choose one of the many blocks from this chapter to stop a bully from robbing you of your power, peace, and purpose. You can take control of the situation instead of leaving the situation, dumbfounded by someone's lack of respect or ignorance. You can protect your positivity and recover more quickly from these BS throwers. In the next chapter you may want to adopt some techniques that will help you ward off predatory behavior and harness even more of your power by speaking your truth. But first, your orange belt test.

Belt Test: Orange to Green (#badassbelttest)

You've done really great work during this chapter, and I'm sure it wasn't easy. Your orange belt test is about celebrating you and your new ease with setting boundaries. To pass your test, you will master the art of blocking the bullshit from your life so it becomes easier and easier for you in your future.

START YOUR TEST

Because so much of our work in this book is to let go of past struggles in order to unleash your mojo, you will work through a confrontation in your past that still haunts you today.

Warning: This exercise can be uncomfortable depending on the scenarios you choose. Always choose to work through the lightest situations first, and save the more heavily charged instances for when you have more practice.

1. Think of a time when you were thrown a heaping pile of BS but instead of blocking with power, you either froze, fled, or fought and wished you had done something different. The purpose here is not to judge your actions, but to accept that you did the best you could in that circumstance and understand that you now have more options available to you if and when you find yourself in a similar situation. Now, that's powerful!

2. Thinking about that instance, consider which strategies you could have used for a different outcome. Could you have created distance from that person altogether? Could you have used one of the soft blocks from this chapter? Or would a hard block have been a better way to handle the situation? Visualize yourself running through the scenario with the newfound powerful block that you choose.

3. Repeat with as many situations from your past that still make you cringe when you think about them.

Bonus points: Is there anywhere in your life where you are playing the bully? Have you been unsupportive of a colleague that could really use your mentoring? Have you been insecure in a relationship and demeaned the person instead of coming clean about your insecurities? Is there any bullshit that you are unnecessarily throwing at some undeserving person? After reading this chapter, is there a behavior you might like to change?

Congratulations! You have passed your belt test and you are now a green belt! 🏯

CHAPTER FOUR

Green Belt: Find Your Roar

An avid runner in her thirties, Kelly Herron was training in a park one day in Seattle when she stopped to use the restroom. When she came out of the stall, she saw that a man had followed her inside. She instinctively knew that what was about to happen was not going to be good and sure enough, he attacked her. She was thrown to the ground and found herself in the fight of her life.

Weeks earlier she was lucky enough to have taken a self-defense class. The lessons came to her all at once: be loud and fight hard! As she fought off her attacker, she screamed a battle cry as loud as she could: "Not today, motherfucker!" Not only did this signal her attacker that she did not come to play, but it also got the attention of a bystander who came to her aid. Together, they locked the predator in a bathroom stall until the cops came and arrested him.

Kelly found her roar when she most needed it. This chapter will help you find your voice and communicate in a powerful way, whether it is to set boundaries, ask for the equal pay you deserve, or anything else worthy of your spirited roar.

What It Means to Be a Green Belt

Green belts in martial arts start to find power in their voice. They begin to deepen their "kihap," the spirited yell used to punctuate a punch or kick. "Ki," which is your energy, and "hap," meaning to harmonize or amplify, the kihap can amplify energy and sounds more like a battle cry. Whether yelling "kihap" or "hiyah" (like Miss Piggy), the intent is to intimidate an opponent while generating more power in your body and spirit. In the beginning, it can feel a bit odd to make these strange sounds, but after much practice, green belts find their groove.

Have you ever not spoken up in class or at a business meeting because you didn't think what you had to say was important enough? Did you ever leave a party and wish you had just asked for his or her number? Do you wish you could have more confidence when you share about your passions, your work, or your mission? If you're not putting yourself and your ideas out there because of a lack of confidence, then it's time to step onto that mat and harness the power of your voice.

At green belt level, you'll find your voice and let the world hear you roar. Your voice is not just the noise that comes from your throat, it's how you move through this world and interact with it and others. It's a tool that you can use to create your dream life by asking for what you want and claiming what you deserve.

Unless you were a communications major in college or have taken some sort of media training, it's likely you have never been taught how to communicate in a powerful way. We learn grammar and punctuation in school but not presentation style.

Maybe a parent told us to stop slouching, but that's not the same as understanding the real importance of body language. Perhaps a parent told us to stop whining but didn't teach us that certain tones and inflections make it more likely that we will be tuned out, viewed as immature, or deemed inexperienced. We learned vocabulary in school, but we probably never realized how words can be emotionally charged and how they can affect our moods. Most importantly, we weren't taught about our inner voice and how much power it can give or take away from us, if we let it.

So, how did we learn how to communicate? Most likely by imitating others around us, like parents, siblings, teachers, or friends. This can be a positive thing if you were surrounded by confident, self-aware people. If not, you may still be hanging on to learned ways of communicating that no longer serve you. But that ends here. Let's level up your voice so people listen and know that you did not come to play.

Channel Your Inner Tiger

To learn how to roar, you'll have to channel your inner tiger. Tigers don't have to be reminded that they're powerful. They're the apex predator, the top beast in the food chain. In a patriarchal society, most women have only experienced being prey and not the predator. We've been conditioned to speak when spoken to and always be polite. We don't want to hurt someone's feelings even if they're being a jerk. We've been told not to be too pushy or too loud because it's too masculine and unladylike. That insidious messaging not only has us not sticking up for ourselves, it also makes us question our voice in general. It keeps us from sharing and expressing our wants, needs, and desires.

Tigers don't question themselves when they speak. They don't ruminate on something they said the day before. They don't sugarcoat things to sound more likeable, and they certainly don't silence their needs because they want to be polite. When you need to assert yourself for any reason, BE THE DAMN TIGER. They saunter and use powerful body language because they're comfortable in their own fur. When they need to roar, they use an unshakeable tone and no-nonsense vocabulary. I'm pretty sure every other animal knows that their ROAR means, "Get the hell out of my way before I eat you!"

We all want to be heard. We all want to communicate in a powerful way. We all have messages within us that can make a positive impact on the people around us. I'm sure there have been times in your life when you've been ignored, passed over, or misunderstood and that's really frustrating. I also bet there have been times in your life when you have communicated in a powerful way. There may be some areas of your life where you are more comfortable communicating than others. Perhaps you're comfortable communicating at home with your family, but in front of your work colleagues, you clam up when you have to present. Or maybe you're a boss in the office but you have trouble expressing yourself on a date. Now is the time to level up all forms of your communication in all areas of your life so you can unleash your impact on the world. Channel the same ferocity of a tiger into your voice when you need to assert yourself or spread your message or your mission.

Stand Tall, Sister

Body language silently communicates on your behalf. It's nonverbal communication, meaning the way you sit, stand, and walk through this world, can be read as a language by others around you.

Feeling sad, down, or even depressed? Chances are your shoulders will be rounded, your spine will be slumped, and your chin will be tilted down. Feeling happy, confident, and alert? Most likely your spine will be straight, your shoulders are back, and your head is held high. Body language is the first thing people notice about you, so before you spend twenty minutes applying your makeup and doing your hair, spend five seconds intentionally setting your body language for the day.

So often we unconsciously hold our bodies in positions that convey negative emotions. We walk through the streets with our heads down and buried in our phones. Not only is this dangerous (watch out for that bus!), it conveys to others that you're not alert and aware of your surroundings. You might even become a prime target for a predator.

People make unconscious assumptions about you from the minute you step into their visual field. Whether you're walking into your boss's office or getting a customer's drink order at the bar, if your shoulders are slumped and your head is facing downward, people assume that you are not feeling confident, happy, or engaged.

If you want to convey confidence, use badass body language. Even if you aren't feeling it in the moment, because *it works both ways.* We all know intuitively that our posture is affected when we feel down. But did you know that you can improve your mood by adjusting your posture? Yes! You can trick yourself into feeling more confident, more alert, and happier by changing your physiology.

Harvard researcher Amy Cuddy, author of the book *Presence*, ran experiments where she put people in power poses. My favorite is called the Wonder Woman: stand up, feet slightly wider than hip-width apart, and hands in fists at your hips. She learned that testosterone levels increased (good for confidence) and cortisol (stress hormone) decreased after holding a power pose for two minutes. The bottom line is that the way you hold your body can actually change your body chemistry! That is powerful stuff.

Using powerful body language is something that I've practiced so often that now it's just how I normally carry myself: shoulders back and head held high. On the mat, it signals that you are alert and ready to train. On the street or in the boardroom, it conveys alertness and confidence. I often travel alone to deliver my keynote speeches and training programs. When I'm in a desolate parking garage late at night or a hotel hallway by myself, I bust out my powerful posture and walk with purpose. I feel more confident, and it can ward off predatory jerks.

Before speaking at a conference, you can find me backstage striking a Wonder Woman pose or strutting around the venue before the audience arrives, marking my territory. Then, before I begin my keynote, I think of Susie from *The Marvelous Mrs. Maisel* saying "Tits up" to Midge before she takes the stage at her comedy shows. This helps me straighten up my spine, set my mental state, and channel my inner tiger. Instead of letting my worry and anxiousness take over, I take charge. Strut, saunter, stand tall, and stick that chest out. Use your body as the powerful weapon it is!

OYH Exercise: Master Your Body Language

1. Check in with your body right now. If you're sitting while reading this book, sit up as straight as you can.

2. Picture a string running up through your spine and out the top of your head.

3. Now picture someone pulling that string so there is no more slack and your spine is as long as possible.

4. Squeeze your shoulder blades together. It will feel like you're sticking your chest out. That's right!

5. Take a deep breath, and let it go. Now play with some facial expressions that match the mood you're going for. For example, if you want to feel happy, smile as big and wide as you can. Smiling releases dopamine, endorphins, and serotonin. Dopamine increases feelings of happiness, endorphins act as a mild pain reliever, and serotonin acts as an antidepressant. Don't just wait for it to happen naturally. Smile often. Smile aggressively! It will help change your state instantly. No pill, edible, or drink can act as quickly!

If confidence is what you're after, play with your smile a bit. Squint your eyes slightly and drop your chin, almost as if you know a secret that nobody else knows. Try this the next time you're in a boardroom or meeting, and you'll have everyone wondering, "What does she know that she's not telling us?"

Take Up Space

My mom loves to tell the story of how, when I was about six years old, she would send me into the deli by myself to buy a gallon of milk. I know, it sounds crazy these days, but back then it seemed pretty safe in the suburban town where I grew up. She would give me a few dollars, I'd go buy the milk, and together we would make sure the change was right when I got back to the car. She says it was a lesson in counting money. One day, after buying the milk, I came out of the deli and told my mom that some man tried to cut me in line. The clerk said, "Next," and this guy stepped right in front of me. I told him, "Hey, Mister, I'm next!" as I stepped in front of him and paid the clerk. My height barely cleared the counter then, but it didn't matter to me. This man tried to cut me, and that was unacceptable!

Thinking back to it, he may not have even seen me. I was so small, but in my mind I was six feet tall. My physical size had nothing to do with how I felt inside. I often think back to that little version of myself feeling so big and taking up space in my little world. Over the years, like so many of us, she shrunk and made herself small at times. She didn't speak up when she really wanted to be seen or heard. She didn't think her needs, wants, or wishes mattered. Luckily, I've been able to reconnect with that younger version of myself. That's my hope for you too.

Can you remember a time when you truly spoke your truth? Stuck up for yourself? Or communicated in a really powerful way? Sit with that memory for a few moments. Connect with that version of yourself. Ask yourself if you've been able to honor her spirit by taking up space, or have you shrunk her or dimmed her light? If that light has been dimmed at all, it's time to turn it up. Imagine a dial you can turn up to amplify the power your younger self once displayed. Regardless of where you're at in your life right now, it can always shine brighter. Keep turning. Keep amplifying. Keep taking up space and keep shining.

Tone It Up

Your tone can sometimes be more powerful than the words you choose. When I was grabbed on the street by that jerk, my tone was enough for my predator to change his mind and run.

The words I used didn't matter as much as the way I screamed them. I've also used my tone to make personal connections and build rapport with VIP clients by softening it when appropriate. Volume, pitch, and pacing convey a lot to your audience, so let's go through them one by one to make sure you're using them to enhance what you're saying, not undercut it.

1. Volume

Women sometimes shy away from using volume. Growing up you may have been told to be quiet and more ladylike, or maybe volume reminds you of anger. It's more than okay and sometimes necessary to turn up the volume when you want to set a powerful boundary or get excited about something. You wouldn't tell your dog to stop eating your slippers in a soft, sweet voice, would you? If someone is pushing your buttons or trying to take advantage of you, speak to them in the same tone you would speak to a naughty puppy.

If you're on the street and someone gets in your space in a threatening way, shout in a deep voice, "Back the fuck up," or "Get out of my space!"

If you're looking to charm a room of potential investors or capture people's attention with a captivating story, play with different ranges of volume throughout to keep it interesting. Go high volume to wake people up, and drop it low when you want them to lean in and listen.

2. Pitch Perfect

People often connect with you, or don't, based on your tone or pitch, the highness or lowness of your voice. We all have a natural pitch that we speak in, but we can also play with pitch to convey strength and power when we want to.

A high pitch can convey nervousness. A deeper pitch has been shown to get people's attention and let them know you're unapologetic and resolute in what you're saying. When negotiating your fees or telling a guy you're not going home with him, drop your pitch and leave no room for questioning. A deeper, lower pitch can be used when you want to set strong boundaries, close a deal, or say something poignant and meaningful. If you're in an office, you may not shout, but you can still convey a serious boundary by dropping your tone. "I am going to HR and reporting your inappropriate behavior," or "Do not speak to me like that ever again."

3. Pace Yourself

Pacing is the speed at which you speak. When we get nervous, we naturally speed up our speech. In our heads we are jumping three thoughts ahead and our mouths are trying to keep up. This comes across as lacking confidence and distracts from our message. The best antidote is to pause and breathe.

I've done this onstage plenty of times when I feel like I'm starting to speed up due to nerves or spiraling thoughts. I remind myself that the audience will still be there when I'm done with my breath. Afterward, I feel calmer, more grounded, and, most importantly, back in the present moment instead of thinking about what I'm going to say three sentences from now. The next time you feel yourself speaking too quickly because your nerves have gotten the best of you, tell yourself to slow down. Breathe. You got this.

On the flip side, when you're genuinely excited about something and you want others to join in that feeling, it is perfectly normal to speed up the pace. Just remember to also slow it down by taking a breath from time to time. Remember, not everyone can keep up!

A note on inflected speech, or when people use certain styles of inflection. Without sounding too harsh, I need to warn you that *uptalk* (a rising inflection at the end or even in the middle of a sentence), *babytalk* (speaking to other adults in a childlike voice), and *vocal fry* (trailing off at the end of a sentence) are ways of speaking that do NOT register well on the "this person is a BOSS and knows what she's talking about" scale. Oftentimes, these styles of speaking were adopted unconsciously as ways of sounding less threatening or to fit in. That's all okay, but your speaking style should be intentional. Check in to be sure that it fits with your current mission of badassery.

Words Will Shape Your World

Your words are powerful. Your words can be used to hurt or to heal. Your words can be used to set boundaries and stick up for yourself and others. Your words can be used to touch, move, and inspire others. Your words can be used to cut off possibilities or create new opportunities. Words are such powerful tools, but we often take them for granted.

When's the last time you said something that you immediately regretted because it damaged the mood or even the relationship? When's the last time that you said something that touched someone so deeply that it made them feel loved, supported, or encouraged? You inherently know how powerful your words are, but at green belt level, it's time to be even more intentional about the words you speak to others and yourself. This can change your life. I know because it's changed mine. I went from a personal trainer to an international public speaker all because of how I have used my voice and my words to speak my truth.

The words you choose to speak out loud shape your world. The same is true of the words we speak to ourselves. The voice in our head that so many of us feel we have no control over, the whispers that tell us that we're not good enough or worthy enough, those words matter too. Many of us are on autopilot when it comes to our negative self-talk and disempowering vocabulary, so much so that we don't realize the impact it has on our confidence. We're not aware how our words attract or repel people, how they stop us from taking risks, or even the energetic frequency they have.

Once I started my personal development work in my early twenties, I began to realize the power of words and their energetic effect on me. Not only did I become more aware of the words I speak, but I became more aware of the messages around me. I stopped listening to music that degraded women. I stopped throwing around the word "hate" unless I really meant it. In general, I became more intentional about what I let in my ears and what came out of my mouth. Do I still put my foot in my mouth? Absolutely. But I now do my best to think twice about the impact my words will have, and, if I do slip up, I use the choices in this chapter to clean up my missteps. When it comes to cleaning up my self-talk, it's an ongoing journey of recognizing and replacing thoughts and words to support my mind and spirit with as much power and self-love as I can in the moment.

Let's go on a deep dive to become more masterful in both our outer and inner vocabulary.

The first step toward more intentional communication is

always awareness. Start becoming more aware and mindful of your conversations with others. Think back to the last few conversations you've had. Do you remember feeling any hints of guilt or shame for things you said? Did you say anything that wasn't true, that may have been hearsay or downright gossip? Did you criticize, make fun of, or demean something or someone? Did you needlessly complain? Did you notice if your contribution to the conversation uplifted others or muted the mood? Without judgment, just observe.

How about in how you communicate on social media or other public forums? Are you mindful of your posts and comments that you put out for the world to see? In general, when I post or comment I think of who will be reading this and what the impact will be. Does it move the conversation forward? Does it add a unique perspective to the conversation? Is there a better way to express myself without resorting to negatively charged vocabulary? If it doesn't meet the criteria of moving the conversation forward, I think twice about posting it.

When in doubt about speaking your mind, especially on a controversial topic, think of this Rumi quote: "Before you speak, let your words pass through three gates. At the first gate, ask yourself 'Is it true?' At the second gate, ask 'Is it necessary?' At the third gate, ask 'Is it kind?'"

Exercise: A Vocabulary Detox

This is not the latest celebrity diet fad. A detox of your speech is more helpful to your badassery than any restrictive food cleanse will ever be. Eliminating certain words and phrases from our speech can elevate our vibe. Speaking poorly about others and ourselves robs us of our power and conveys a lack of confidence and self-esteem.

For the next seven consecutive days, practice the following steps. They aren't easy, but you will be rewarded by becoming more aware of how your words affect your world.

1. Drop the self-deprecation: There's a difference between a little self-deprecation to bring humor or humility to a conversation and outright talking crap about yourself. I've witnessed (and been a part of) this many times in my past. It spreads like wildfire. One woman will start saying something like, "Ugh, I'm so bloated. I've gained so much weight over the holidays. My stomach is rolling over my jeans." And sure enough, a friend will jump in and say something like, "No, you look amazing. *I'm disgusting*! Look at these wrinkles and my gray hair is coming in." Can we stop this vicious cycle, please? It feeds a competition of negative self-talk that only affirms our self-doubt.

Practice: If you find yourself in a conversation with someone who is talking negatively about herself, and you're about to do the same, change the subject. If you really want the behavior to stop, call it out in an encouraging way and make an agreement to collectively stop. Say something like, "Anna, I really value our friendship. Every time we get together, we get in a cycle of negative self-talk, and I'm doing my best to limit mine. Would you be willing to make a pact going forward to stop talking smack about ourselves?"

2. Quit gossiping: Our outward language about other people carries a positive or negative charge. Nobody wants to be around the person who's constantly knocking others because you know that person will eventually be talking about you too. It may seem innocuous in the moment, but slagging on others makes you look bad, not them. Instead, be the person who is generous with her compliments. The more positive words you put into the universe, the more they will come back to you.

Practice: If you've just committed a gossip crime, go ahead and call yourself out. Say something like "You know what? That was mean, and I'd like to take that back." Then, if it feels authentic, point out something positive about the person. The more you call yourself out about your gossiping, the less you're going to want to do it.

3. Avoid disaster statements: *The world is going to shit. Life is hard. Love is a battlefield. My career is in the toilet. Weight loss is impossible.* These types of over-the-top exaggerations paint our perceptions in very dramatic and unnecessary ways. When I hear clients use this kind of language, I know there's work to do to break down ways of thinking that are blocking possibilities of a brighter future.

Practice: Anytime you use a disaster statement, use a counter question to help you realize how true or untrue your statements are. You do it by simply repeating the statement as a question. For example, if you say, "People are assholes," a good counter question could be, "Are all people really assholes?" Of course, they aren't! There are tons of great people in this world. If you're looking to avoid disaster statements, you can say something more specific like, "Some people really shock me with their behavior, and specifically, this particular person acted like an asshole."

4. Ditch filler words: Filler words are often unconsciously used to fill the space when we can't complete our thought or are used to punctuate one. They can be distracting and can make you sound unsure of yourself. The challenge is that they come out of our mouths so unintentionally most of the time and are difficult to catch.

Common filler words to be on the lookout for:

- Ums, uhs, ahs, ers
- Like, you know, I mean
- Okay, so, actually
- Right?
- Oh my God
- Basically, literally

Practice: The first step is to recognize which filler words you use on a regular basis. The next time you have a conversation with someone, simply become more aware of what you're saying, and see if you tend to use particular filler words. When you find them, start slowing down your speech just a bit and be more intentional with your words. Whenever you start hearing yourself using one, close your mouth, take a breath, and skip to the next sentence or thought. This will clean up your talk, help you get to the point more quickly, and enroll others in your ideas in a more powerful way.

4. End the exaggerations: Most of us have a real tendency to exaggerate our feelings. Feelings are valid, but it's also important to remember they aren't facts. They don't have power over you; you control them. When I catch myself starting to say things like *I feel like absolute shit, I'm devastated,* or *I'm hopeless,* I check in with myself to see how much of it I'm really feeling and how much I'm exaggerating by using the exaggeration scale. This technique puts things into perspective and can help you choose different, less intense words to describe your feelings.

THE EXAGGERATION SCALE

Step 1: Identify the disaster word or phrase you used to describe your feelings.

Step 2: Ask yourself, on a scale of 1 to 10, how {fill in the blank} am I really? Check in with yourself and be honest.

Step 3: If the number is less than 8, perhaps there's a different, less loaded word to choose to describe your feelings.

Example: I was devastated by the fight I just had with my best friend.

Step 1: "Devastated" is the disaster word.

Step 2: On a scale of 1 to 10, how devastated am I really? My first gut reaction is more like a 5. Therefore, maybe I'm not really devastated.

Step 3: Maybe I'm more sad or disappointed. Sad and disappointed feel less charged than devastated. When a situation can be reframed with language that isn't so disastrous or exaggerated, we have easier access to our logical thoughts. From there, we can come up with better solutions and coping mechanisms to deal with the situation.

Power-Draining vs. Power-Gaining Vocabulary

Sometimes the most innocuous phrases, especially the ones we say on repeat, can be like mini power drains, slowly zapping us of our power. You may use the following words and phrases quite often and don't even realize the impact of them.

The following are examples of power-draining phrases and power-gaining swaps.

Swap "I should have, would have, or could have" for "I now choose to." The words *should've, would've,* and *could've* all live in the past. There is no power in the past. There's no way to go back and change it. Focus on the present moment and what you will choose to do going forward. This helps you take back your power from lamenting over the past and what you should have done then.

Swap "I'll try" with "I will or will not do a particular thing." The word *try* implies that your participation is optional, which takes power away from your commitment. When clients say to me that they will try to cook healthy meals, work out, or ask for a raise, I know they are not fully committed to the outcome. They are wavering on their commitment because they either don't believe they can do it or it's not a priority. Yoda said it best: "Do or do not. There is no try."

Swap "I'm just following up" with "I am following up." The word *just* feels like an apology. It minimizes us and lessens the power of our presence. Say what you are actually doing, not what you're *just* doing.

Swap "I've got 99 problems" with "I have 99 challenges, obstacles, or opportunities for growth." A *problem* implies negativity whereas *challenges, obstacles,* and *opportunities* feel like solutions are possible. The next time you're about to say you have a problem, try one of the other three options and see how powerful you feel about coming up with a solution.

Swap "but" with "and." When we use the word *but* to connect two thoughts, it can take the power and possibility out of the second thought. For example, have you ever said to your partner, "You've done a great job cleaning out the basement, *but* you missed the closet"? The *but* makes your original intention to praise the work your partner has done way less powerful. Or perhaps you're dating someone or interviewing a great candidate for a position and you say, "He's really smart but he could use some work on his wardrobe." Try swapping that *but* for an *and.* "He's really smart AND he can use some work on his wardrobe." Now it feels like there is more possibility. Both statements can be true and coexist.

Swap "Sorry" with "Excuse me." Stop apologizing all the time! Women especially have a bad habit of overapologizing, and we need to cut it out. Men do not do this. Men are generally not apologetic for their presence in this world, and they certainly don't verbalize it constantly. The next time you're about to say sorry for something that doesn't deserve an apology, either say nothing or, if appropriate, an "Excuse me" will do. If you're about to interrupt a conversation when something is urgent, say "Excuse me." When you need to pass someone in the hallway who is taking up a ton of space, "Excuse me." If you're saying sorry for expressing yourself, then shut the sorry down.

I was often at the gym at the same time as this woman, let's call her Janet, who would be doing her exercises in the same general area as me. We always smiled and acknowledged each other.

Immediately after the greeting, she would apologize for being in my space. There was plenty of space to share, so I never understood what she meant. Each time she apologized, I would tell her that she wasn't in my way. Every. Single. Time. And she still never stopped. One day it hit me: Janet has probably been apologizing to people all her life for simply taking up space! Why do we feel like taking up space in this world is something we have to apologize for?

Stop apologizing for telling jokes, for being tired, for laughing uncontrollably, for spreading joy, for interrupting when it's important, for showing up in someone's inbox, for being bumped into, for using your voice, for standing up for yourself, or for standing up for others. Stop apologizing unless something you have intentionally done has hurt another person.

Self-Talk: Stop the Self-Sabotage!

We spent the orange belt chapter blocking bullshit coming from other people, but for many of us, the voice inside our own head can be worse than even the rudest comment sent flying in our direction. And the worst part is that our negative internal voice isn't as easy to block because it's insidious in nature; it becomes part of our inner dialogue on repeat. According to the National Science Foundation, an average person has about 50,000 thoughts per day. Of those, about 80 percent are negative. Imagine how many of those negative thoughts are about yourself, your abilities, your talents, your personality, your body, your work, or your relationships. With all those negative thoughts, we're programming our minds to set us up for failure.

Whether your negative internal voice is calling you out as an imposter, or it rags on your body, or it tells you you aren't enough, it's getting in your way of being your best self. It's robbing you of power and peace and keeping you from your purpose. These negative thoughts are like tiny seeds planted by a patriarchal and sometimes shallow society. Every time we allow those thoughts to linger and don't change our thought patterns, we allow them to grow like weeds in our minds; they are weeds that strangle and starve our potential.

Sometimes, everywhere you look, the world is telling you you're not enough. Social media is screaming, "Look how perfect everyone's life is but yours!" Billboards are telling you that you're not cool or thin enough. TV shows are telling you that you need to use humor or sex to get people to like you. Society is telling you that if you're not married with 2.5 kids and a house with a backyard and a nice car by the time you reach your thirtieth birthday, you are an absolute failure. And that our looks dictate our worth, and therefore, as we start to age into our forties, fifties, and beyond, we become less attractive and therefore less worthy.

Enough already! It's time to get out the machete and start weed whacking your internal thought garden. It's time to starve those weeds so they can shrivel and die and to let your badassery thrive. It's time to declare your worth, your power, and your purpose. To carve your own path in society and claim it as your own. And it all starts with transforming your internal dialogue.

Negative thoughts may never go away entirely. Believing so would be extremely Pollyannaish. But the more we can recognize them and separate them from our true and powerful selves, and then replace them with empowering thoughts and internal dialogue, fewer weeds will grow. And the more space we'll have to believe in ourselves, value ourselves, practice self-care, and contribute our gifts to the world. You don't need to become a Zen master to accomplish this; it just takes practice. And just like with all the other exercises in this book, practice becomes a way of being. It's not something you do once or twice and are done with it. Our internal dialogue is a continuous work in progress. We'll slip up and we'll begin again. Over time, the slip-ups happen less, and we become masters of our own mind.

Exercise: Machete Time

To start changing up the negative self-talk, walk through the following five steps.

1. Discovery

Ask yourself what are the most negative things you say to yourself? Remember times when you stopped yourself from expressing yourself. Maybe you stopped wearing a dress you once loved or chose not to say what was on your mind. Find situations where you've stopped yourself from following a dream or a passion. Go to those moments in your memory and listen to the thoughts that come up for you. Hint: Often those negative thoughts stopping us from expressing our power include the words "not enough." For example, I'm not smart enough to go back to school. I'm not experienced enough to apply for that job. I'm not thin enough to wear that dress. I'm not doing, being, or having enough. I'm not enough. Period.

When you hear that voice, tune in. Notice the specific words and phrases it uses. You may recognize some of those words and phrases from memories buried deep in your past. Perhaps they were said to you by a mean uncle, an abusive coach, or jealous frenemy. Or they may be things you decided were true about yourself when you had the brain of a child. Surely you don't need to hang on to thoughts that you had about yourself at five, ten, or fifteen years old. You're the grown-up now. You're in charge, and you get to choose which thoughts will serve and support you and which need to get weed whacked with your mental machete.

The next time you hear those thoughts begin to surface, recognize the voice. Notice the voice, and if you can place where it comes from, recognize that too. If not, that's okay. Keep going with the exercise.

2. Stop them in their tracks

Stop the thoughts before they begin to spiral by acknowledging the voice. You can even talk to it. You can say something like "Hi. Thanks for sharing but I'm in charge now."

3. Machete time

Picture yourself taking out your machete and chopping these weeds at the root, killing them off.

4. Rewrite and replace

Now replace those thoughts with new, positive, supportive ones. Thoughts that will help you sprout new possibility and grow deep and sturdy roots. Flip the negative thoughts into the exact opposite positive solution. These are the seeds you're planting so they can begin to take up more mental space as you grow. They will help support you on your toughest days and be there to boost your smooth ones. Here are examples of common negative thoughts turned into positive counterparts:

- "I'm not worthy of {fill in the blank}" replaced with "I am worthy. I deserve the accolades, the position, the money I earn, etc."

- "I'm unlovable" replaced with "I am lovable. I am worthy of all the love and affection every single day."
- "I'm not pretty enough" replaced with "I am a gorgeous goddess. My body is strong. My external shell is a reflection of my beauty within."
- "I'm not desirable / I'm too fat / I'm too thin" replaced with "I am desirable. I attract the perfect people into my life who love and support me."
- "I'm not smart enough" replaced with "I am intelligent. I am creative. I have the ability to tap into an unlimited creative source on demand."
- "I'm not rich enough" replaced with "I am wealthy. I have a home. I have an abundance of friends, food to eat, and love in my life."
- "I'm not young enough," aka I am too late / too old, replaced with "My timing is perfect. My life is divinely planned, and everything happens at the exact right time."
- "I'm not disciplined enough" replaced with "I am laser focused on the things that are important to me and that help me advance my dreams and desires."

Note: When rewriting your thoughts, make sure they sound and feel good to you. Make sure they feel aligned with the person you're becoming. If they feel like downright lies, you may dismiss them. Choose words and phrases that feel beyond where you are right now but represent the direction you are heading toward, the direction of your true badassery.

5. Put it on repeat

Say these statements as often as possible on repeat. Say them to yourself, and say them out loud when you're in the shower or driving in your car. Say them immediately following a negative thought or when you're feeling down in the dumps. Allow them to evoke the feelings of your new positive statements. Bask in those feelings and allow them to seep into your pores and bathe your cells with badassery.

As I write these words, I hear my internal negative voice. It tells me that this book is not good enough. That I'm not smart enough. That nobody will care and I suck at writing. So, I stop and acknowledge the voice. I thank it for sharing, maybe even for helping me strive to become a better writer. Then I get out my mental machete and whack the hell out of those weeds. I replace them with, "I am writing to one woman out there who will hear these words and be inspired to change her thoughts for more power and peace in her life. I am creative. I have the ability to tap into an unlimited source of creativity. My style of writing is unique and authentic to me." This gives me the courage to continue.

> "Watch your thoughts; they become words.
> Watch your words; they become actions. Watch your actions;
> they become habit. Watch your habits; they become character.
> Watch your character; it becomes your destiny."
> —Lao Tzu

Belt Test: Green to Blue (#badassbelttest)

You have leveled up your communication skills in a powerful way. Now it's time to finally become a master of your own voice. Your green to blue belt test is the ultimate exercise in proving to yourself that you are in control of your thoughts and your words.

START YOUR TEST: BUILD YOUR BATTLE CRY

Every woman deserves her own battle cry. When you're on a mission and just don't have time for the nonsense, having a battle cry can carry you through life like a warrior. A battle cry is like your positive thought exercise on steroids. It's a phrase that you'll use to remind yourself how badass you are when your life feels like a battle. Kelly Herron used "Not today, motherfucker" to defend herself against an actual predator. You can use your battle cry to get you through whatever life throws your way.

1. Head back to the Machete Time exercise where you wrote down all the negative thoughts you say to yourself about your worth, your intelligence, your body, or anything that you judge about yourself in a negative way.

2. Choose three to five of the negative statements that sting the most and carry the most weight. Find their positive counterpart.

3. Write them into a powerful paragraph. Be creative with your words and phrases. I suggest putting your paragraph on a sticky note and placing it on your bathroom mirror so you can see yourself as you speak your truth out loud.

4. Stand in a power pose. Separate your legs slightly wider than hip-width apart. Place your hands on your hips in fists or put them up in the air.

5. Read your battle cry out loud in a deep, powerful tone.

6. Repeat five times until it sinks in and feels great in your body and spirit.

Use this battle cry daily. It's a powerful way to start your day. Say it to yourself throughout the day whenever you're feeling pressured or stressed, and say it before you head to sleep at night to fill your subconscious mind with powerful thoughts.

My battle cry is:

I am strong. I am safe. I am powerful beyond measure. I am healthy. I am wealthy. I am loving and generous. I am unstoppable on my mission to help others feel strong, safe, and powerful from the streets to the boardroom.

Congratulations on letting the world hear you roar! And welcome to your blue belt level.

CHAPTER FIVE

Blue Belt:
Elevate Your Energy

My last year living in New York City, I was a hot mess. I wanted to make as much money as I could to pay for my NYC rent and grad school, so this meant I had to take on as many clients as I could possibly pack into a full day. At the same time, I was pursuing a master's degree in nutrition and trying to enjoy a social life. Each morning, I would drag myself out of bed and down into the subway before dawn to get to my clients' homes to train them, puffy eyes and all. After a few sessions, I'd go back home to study or head to the dojo for class. By the afternoon, I would pass out for an hour or two. Then I'd drag myself to the dojo (again) to train more clients, teach class, take a class, and practice some more. Some days I would be on the mat for five hours, plus a few more hours at clients' homes. Afterward, I would meet friends for wine and comfort food, go to bed, and repeat the next day. It was a haze of caffeine-fueled days, soul-crushing subway rides, and wine-filled nights, pushing my body to its limits physically.

I was a personal trainer, a health coach, and a martial arts instructor. I was coaching others to nourish their bodies, minds, and spirits, yet I was a walking zombie. I was headed for a well-being breakdown, and I needed to do something drastic to get my life back on track.

It was a bleak and freezing-cold day in NYC when I called my friend Michelle to vent. She described her current situation in Venice, California, working from her "tree house" as she called it, sitting on her sun-drenched porch with her dog, Jack. She invited me to visit and I jumped at the chance. I was on a plane the next week.

During that week, I felt my energy coming back slowly but surely. For the first time in a while, my spirit lit up as I started to swoon over the flower-lined streets of Venice and the views of the Santa Monica Mountains. I wound up booking a second trip to LA within a few short weeks, this time for a six-week stint. It was then that I truly began healing myself from the inside out. My "Jenn energy" was coming back as I began letting go of sadness and cynicism and actively cultivating more positivity, motivation, and vitality. I started taking better care of my body, my nutrition, and my lifestyle and watched as my energy returned. I avoided burnout by taking a reset and reprioritizing my health and self-care.

We all experience energy drain, but you don't have to be passive when it happens. No matter what you're going through in life, you can reclaim your power starting today. You can reboot and supercharge your life with energy, vitality, and pure badassery.

What It Means to Be a Blue Belt

Becoming a blue belt in martial arts requires self-reflection and a shift in focus from the outward to the inward. The blue belt begins to understand how deeply connected the mind and body are. In order to keep up one's strength, blue belts must manage their energy and keep it balanced naturally instead of looking to artificial sources to fuel it.

In Eastern philosophies this energy has a name. The names differ according to language: *chi* or *qi* in Chinese, *ki* in Japanese, *prana* in Sanskrit. They all refer to the life force energy that gives us vitality and unites our mind, body, and spirit. There are whole systems of exercises geared toward developing this energy, including tai chi, qi gong, and different forms of breathwork and meditation.

In Western culture, we barely acknowledge that this energy exists. We go through life doing as much as we can in order to achieve as much as we can, in order to hopefully retire one day with as much stuff as we can. Along the way, many of us get stuck and even sick because we've been drained of so much of our life-giving energy. We do have a name for that. It's called burnout.

A Gallup study of nearly 7,500 full-time employees found that 23 percent of employees reported feeling burned out at work very often or always, while an additional 44 percent reported feeling burned out sometimes. That means about two-thirds of full-time workers experience burnout on the job. (And that was pre-COVID-19.) At work, this results in more sick days, lower job retention, and lower confidence in performance. What's more difficult to measure is the toll it takes on other parts of life: relationships, mental health, and physical health.

How can you cultivate a fun, sexy relationship if you're dragging your ass out of bed every morning? How can you be a fully present parent to your kids if you're sleepwalking through the day? How can you feel connected to your job, business, or life's mission if you're counting down the minutes until you can clock out for wine time? At some point it will catch up with you.

At the pace we're going, it's no wonder many of us are heading for burnout. Women take on more chores in a heterosexual, partnered household according to a Gallup poll. Women also tend to take on more responsibility when it comes to childcare. Trying to balance a fast-paced career, social obligations, family life, and your 401K can be difficult enough. Throw a traumatic event into the mix, and it's like a lit match heading for a bundle of dry twigs. It's inferno city. No amount of green juice or other Goop-endorsed products will give you the energy to deal with your life like a warrior. Handling stress becomes grueling. Life feels like a grind. Your body bears the burden.

Physically, your immune system becomes insufficient, which means more susceptibility to colds and viruses. Chronic aches and pains can manifest from inflammation. Stress hormones like cortisol and adrenaline are being pumped out into your body constantly. They wreak havoc on your endocrine system and can keep unwanted weight on even if you're doing all the "right" things to take it off.

Stress and anxiety build and take up more and more mental space, like a squatter who won't pay the rent. Depression rates have increased severely in millennials according to a study by Blue Cross Blue Shield in 2019, and they are seeing their physical and mental health decline at a faster rate than Gen Xers as they age. More social media, more news, more expenses, more pressure—it all adds up, and without the proper coping skills and lifestyle modifications, this pressure can feel like Mount Vesuvius ready to explode. But instead of spewing lava, you find yourself at the doctor's office with difficult-to-diagnose issues like extreme fatigue, digestion problems, headaches, weird rashes, or insomnia. The doctor will give you a pill to patch up the symptom, but if no lifestyle changes are made, the volcano will erupt in other ways.

My goal for you in this chapter is that you make the proper lifestyle changes before you faceplant at the office or become sick. The good news is we can reverse this process and heal our mind and body while elevating our energy. Let's face it, we need all the energy we can get to live our most badass lives. As a blue belt, you'll create a holistic battle plan to take control over your well-being once and for all.

What's Draining Your Energy?

From food, to frenemies, to overpacked schedules, to mountains of stress, there are so many variables in our lives that are depleting our energy. Visualize yourself surrounded by an energetic bubble. A bubble of chi. This bubble acts like a shield to protect your energy, power, and peace. Over the years, little pin holes have been made in your energetic bubble, and slowly, your energy has been leaking out. Your energy bubble may even look like a pincushion about to be flat-out deflated. We'll start building your holistic battle plan by identifying your energy leaks so you can plug them up and stop the drain.

After fifteen years of coaching clients to better health and well-being, I've noticed patterns in energetic drains. When life gets the most hectic, we neglect our self-care when we need it most. Many of us are relying on the same vices to get us through the most stressful times in life. As obvious as the following list may seem to you, I'm always surprised by women who know better, but still allow these habits to drain their energy. In moderation they're harmless. But over time, if not checked, these power drains leave us zapped of our energy, happiness, and sometimes, our health.

Coffee Crazed

That first cup of delicious brew in the morning tastes so good and can help wake you up. I sometimes even start looking forward to it before I go to sleep the night before. However, I see too many women relying on too many lattes to get them through their day.

Too much caffeine overstimulates the adrenal glands, which are responsible for secreting those stress hormones I mentioned back in orange belt. When you're stressed out your body needs the opposite. It needs to recover and recalibrate from the stress induced by your packed schedule and on-the-go lifestyle. Slugging Venti cold brew all day may feel like it's giving you the energy you need to hit your deadlines, but it's slowly causing wear and tear to your mind and body, overloading it with cortisol and other stress hormones.

HOW DO YOU KNOW IF YOU'RE DRINKING TOO MUCH CAFFEINE?

Ask yourself the following questions:

1. Do I rely on caffeine to help get me through my day? If the answer is yes, go deeper. Look for the root causes of your

lack of energy. Hopefully, by the end of this chapter, you'll have your answers!

2. At what point does caffeine start to make me jittery? Stop before you get to that point.

3. How much caffeine do I need to get me through the afternoon? Try having one less than that.

4. Do I have trouble falling asleep or staying asleep at night? If yes, cut way back on your total caffeine and cut it off by at least noon to give it ample time to metabolize and leave your body, which can take up to eight hours in some people!

Slowly but surely, cut back on excess caffeine and watch your energy rise again over time.

Wine Time

Have you ever lied to your doctor about how many alcoholic drinks you have per week? Been there! Look, a glass or two of wine at dinner with friends or a margarita at happy hour that amplifies your happiness and adds to the celebratory vibe can outweigh the inflammatory effects alcohol has on the body or the energy slump you may feel the next day.

You may feel like a drink or two after work helps take the edge off, but for some people, alcohol can make it more difficult to process stress and worsen feelings of depression and anxiety. Alcohol can disrupt sleep cycles, not allowing your body to feel fully recharged in the morning, which sets you up to compensate with copious amounts of caffeine. Alcohol can also lead to more mindless food choices. It's harder to say no to the side of fries after a glass of rosé.

Check in with yourself and ask how you feel while drinking, and the day after drinking? If you're experiencing "hangxiety" more often than you'd like, if you're relying on alcohol to numb out or to escape reality, then it's a bigger problem than it's worth. When it starts to disrupt your life, your health, or your relationships it's time to hit the pause button.

Sweet Tooth

Anyone who has ever struggled with their weight knows that sugar is not their friend, but have you considered how it affects your energy and mental health? When sugar, in all its processed forms, is eaten, it lights up the pleasure center of the brain and releases feel-good chemicals like dopamine. This feeling makes you crave even more. Just one more spoonful of ice cream, I swear! And the next thing you know you've finished the pint. Over time your body needs more and more to get that same great feeling, aka a sugar high. Sugar sends our bodies on a blood sugar roller coaster which can make feelings of depression and anxiety worse.

The food industry knows our weakness for sugar so they add it to everything from bread to vitamins, as well as all the obvious foods like your morning cereal and chocolate bars. Large food corporations care about their bottom line, not your bottom and not your brain. They want to sell more food, so they prey on your brain's ability to become addicted to sugar. Breaking the addiction of sugary foods can be tricky, but it's completely possible. And when you do, you take that power back from sugar and big food corporations. Back into your own hands so you can feel great naturally, without mood swings, blood sugar spikes, or a fatty liver.

Comfort Foods

Mac 'n' cheese. Ice cream. Flamin' Hot Cheetos. Gooey. Creamy. Sweet and salty. Foods that are so processed and loaded with enough preservatives to survive the zombie apocalypse are draining your energy slowly and surely. What may feel like a burst of energy or pleasure in the moment is really causing blood sugar imbalances that can lead to mood swings, difficulty focusing, and even disease.

Comfort foods may already fall under the sugar category for you. Or maybe you're more of a salty snacker. Or you may find comfort in a pizza or french fry binge. If you're relying on comfort foods to numb your pain or soothe your stress, remember that binge may be setting you up to self-sabotage your health goals. Especially if you binge and then restrict afterward. This pattern that I see so often in clients can quickly become a source of guilt, shame, and self-loathing.

Take your power back from the pull that comfort foods have over you. Remember that they are engineered in a way to make you eat more and crave more. Don't beat yourself up. Keep your kitchen filled with foods that fuel your energy, not rob it. Each time you choose to eat whole foods over processed comfort foods, you're building up your power and energy. Over time, you'll feel more confident, and you'll begin to trust yourself to take care of your body like the badass machine it is.

The Negatiuity Uirus

This virus is insidious to your energy tank, and it spreads rapidly from host to host. We can catch this virus from outside sources like the 24/7 news cycle, social media, and Negative Ned from the office. We also breed this virus within ourselves through negative thoughts, speech patterns, and behaviors (like the ones we cleaned up in the last chapter). Let's edge out even more negativity to create space for greater experiences and more badassery.

Body Shame

My dear, you have this one body. A body that was assigned to you at birth. It came with genetics that predetermined to some extent your shape, coloring, and predispositions. There's no trading it in for a different version. There's no point in wishing it were different. It just is. Yet, I hear over and over women shaming their bodies because they don't look like the fake, Photoshopped, unrealistic bodies that we see in the media. And don't get me wrong, I used to do it too. I wished my tummy was flatter, my boobs were bigger, and my nose was smaller. That's until I realized how much power I was giving away and the energy I was wasting. And for what? To please whom? I realized that those ideals of beauty that I was wishing for were not my own. I was brainwashed into thinking I should look a certain way instead of accepting and loving myself for who I am. I no longer have time for that! Instead of shaming my body, I now appreciate it for all that it does for me, and I treat it preciously because it's the only one I have. That's my hope for you too.

Do you speak about your body in a negative way to your partner, friends, family, or yourself? Do you complain about the fat on your stomach, the stretch marks on your thighs, or the birthmark on your skin? Do you point out every new wrinkle on your face or gray hair on your head with disdain? That's when you can stop yourself in your tracks and take that power back.

Where did that shame come from? Did it come from your childhood? A comment about your weight in middle school from a mean girl? The constant comparison of your body to an airbrushed model in a magazine (or on social media today)? Or perhaps, sadly, it has manifested from the violence suffered at the hands of an abuser. None of this is fair or your fault. But the question becomes, do you still want to give power to the source of your shame? That mean girl, advertiser, or abuser? NO. It's time to take that power back where it belongs. For you and the life you want. A life of freedom from body shame. Maybe even a body worth celebrating.

Choose the body that you have right now. Accept it for all that it is and is not. Then take the very best care of it you can. Use all the energy and time you waste on shaming your body for good. Use that time to prep a healthy meal, go for a walk, get a massage, or take a nap. Any time you choose to treat your body well instead of picking it apart, you are cultivating more peace and more power for your life.

Exercise: Break Up with Body Shame

1. Head to the closest mirror.
2. Take a deep breath.
3. Stare into your eyes for at least sixty seconds as you continue to take long, deep breaths.
4. Connect with that warrior within. Say hey.
5. Now that you're present to all her inner strength, start looking at the outer shell, your body. Start to thank your body for all that it does for you. Did it get you out of bed today? Say thanks. Did it walk you in and out of the train, subway, or car today? Say thanks. Did it pick up your child, feed your cat, or call your mom? Say thank you. Your body does so incredibly much for you behind the scenes and never gets an ounce of appreciation. Thank it for all its strength and innate wisdom. Thank it for housing your brain and

your soul. Thank it for never giving up on you even though you may have given up on it.

6. Now make it a promise. If you've been at war with your body, it's time for a truce and a renewal of vows. Promise your body that you'll treat it with more respect going forward. That you won't call it names and feel so shameful in your skin. Promise it you'll start listening more to what it needs, be it food, movement, or sleep.

7. Seal your promise with an air kiss to yourself.

8. Repeat this exercise as often and as much as needed.

24/7 News Cycle

Sure, it's important to be aware of what's going on in your country and in the world, but how much news do we need? Back in the day, we had to read a newspaper or wait to tune into the nightly news. Nowadays, our phones and laptops are pinging us with real-time updates on the latest breaking announcements. Do we really need to know the moment the newest iPhone is released?

Turning off news alerts and setting boundaries on how long you'll leave the news channel on is a strategy to help you from getting sucked into the urgency and the doom and gloom of the talking heads news cycle. I used to get stuck in front of the TV anytime something horrible had happened in this country or globally. Accidents, mass shootings, terrorist attacks, you name it. You couldn't peel me away even though the reporters kept repeating the same story over and over as time went on. Now, I limit myself to one full cycle of news. Meaning once the reporters start repeating stories, it's time to change the channel or shut it off completely. Once I do, I take my power back from the negativity of the news media and choose how I want to feel for the rest of the night.

Social Media

There's no doubt that social media has changed the way we live. I love it for so many reasons. I get to see my friends' children grow up. I get to wish more people a happy birthday. I learn helpful hacks on how to present the perfect cheese plate or how to slice an avocado. I get to connect with more people around the world who I can hopefully help with an inspiring message or make them laugh with a funny picture.

I'm also incredibly thankful that I didn't grow up having social media. I'm happy that I had to fill my time, not scrolling on a phone, but with real-life conversations or playing Uno. There was pressure from the media to look a certain way, but it wasn't in my face 24/7. I had to buy a magazine or watch back-to-back episodes of *Facts of Life* to see enough commercials to have them hold some influence over me. I thought Cindy Crawford and Tyra Banks were stunning, but I wasn't trying to emulate them. I thought heroin chic (thank you, Kate Moss) was unattainable, and I never got sucked into the idea that skinny must = beautiful. But I'm not so sure growing up with today's pressures of social media would be so easy for even the most grounded of us to ignore.

What about us adults though? Shouldn't we be immune to the pressures of social media? You would think so, but I still catch myself in a comparison trap with successful entrepreneurs and their perfect-looking Instagrammable lives. Have you ever asked yourself questions like, "Why don't I have as many followers as her? Why can't my stomach be as flat as hers? Why can't I own a fabulous beach house in Malibu too?" I know I have, and it sounds ridiculous!

Once I start going down the comparison spiral, I know it's time to jump off that train, set some boundaries, and focus my attention elsewhere. Focus on my present reality and all the things I'm grateful for. And you can too. If you really go overboard, you can always head back to your Greatest Hits List to remind yourself of all the achievements you're proud of, regardless of anyone else and theirs.

Exercise: Detox Your Feed

It's time to take your power back from social media and the accounts that you follow that make you feel energy drained. Whether you feel bad about yourself because you don't look like the latest fitness Instagram influencer, or you're feeling inadequate about your career when you compare yourself to others on LinkedIn, do a quick scan of your social media health, find those energy leaks, and plug them up with some unfollows!

Start with the social media account you spend the most time on and follow the prompts. Repeat for any additional social media accounts you have.

1. Open the account and search for any account that makes you feel anything other than inspired, happy, healthy, and grateful. Mute. Unfollow. Unfriend. Unsubscribe. It's really that simple. I don't care if they are your friends or colleagues. Free up that space! After some time, you won't even remember that they once were a power drain.

2. Find accounts that inspire you. Lift you up. Find creators

who help you feel hopeful, empowered, confident, healthy, wealthy, and grateful. I prefer to follow accounts that are authentic and show the lows and not just the highlights. I love accounts that feature good news and people making a difference in the world. I'm not here for perfectly curated, too perfect, or Photoshopped.

3. Curate your social media experience carefully and with discernment. Remember, nobody can make you feel a certain way about yourself, but you can choose to remove the temptation to do so. Once you've crafted a positive social media experience for yourself, you'll gain power and energy from your time on social media instead of being drained by it.

Energy Gains

While you're working on plugging up all those energy leaks, you can also start taking a proactive approach to generating more energy and vitality so you can feel like the badass black belt you're becoming. Whether you're in a season of suck or in the flow, generating more energy can be the start of a healthier lifestyle. The items that follow are not meant to be things you do intensely for a short period of time and then forget about them like a trendy diet. They are ways of being that, when added to your life consistently over time, will bring you more power, peace, and purpose.

Hydrate Like a Champ

I'm always shocked at how many of my clients drink such little amounts of water. If you're one of those people who answers the question of, "How much water do you drink?" with, "Does coffee count?" then it's time to get the watering hose out and power up those cells of yours.

Dehydration has so many ill effects on the body, including fatigue, brain fog, dizziness, headaches, dry skin, and even sugar cravings. It makes sense considering our body is made up of mostly water. Even our brain is made of mostly water (and fat). Yet too many of us ignore the signs of dehydration and continue to slug coffee all day when we really just need a glass of darn water.

The amount of water needed depends on many factors like your weight, activity level, and even the climate you live in (the hotter the climate, the more water you sweat out and therefore need to replace). So, when you hear advice like "drink eight glasses of water a day" as a blanket recommendation, it should raise a red flag. Should a 120-pound woman who sits at her desk all day drink the same amount of water as a 250-pound man who goes to CrossFit five days a week? Clearly, the answer is more nuanced than that.

You'll have to find what works for you, your body, and your lifestyle, but a guide to get you started is to drink about half your body weight in ounces per day:

• Body weight (in pounds)/2 = ounces of water per day

For example: a 150-pound woman would drink about 75 ounces of water daily.

After figuring out your own equation, if it sounds like way too much, then start with less and work your way up. You will pee more. So what? When your pee becomes closer to clear than dark yellow, you know you're hydrating like a champ.

Sleep Like a Star

Silky pajamas, eye masks, and a bed fit for a queen? Yes please! I do not play when it comes to sleep. In fact, I teach my clients to treat their sleep like an Olympic event. Train for it. Prepare for it, and set up your environment to make it as easy and enjoyable as possible. The reward is a better quality of sleep that can help you focus, retain information, heal your body, lose unwanted weight, increase your immunity, and elevate your energy!

So why does sleep get treated like the dying houseplant that you forget to water? It's the last thing that people want to attend to and many of us have just accepted lack of sleep as a way of life. It doesn't help that our society values productivity over rest and recovery. Working well into the evening is somehow still deemed applaudable, and in some cases, expected.

The stress of overworking, outstanding bills, the sickness of a loved one, or the uncertainty of the future all contribute to keeping us up at night. Practicing healthy sleep hygiene, no matter what's happening in your world, can help you fall asleep more quickly and stay asleep longer, giving your body the deep rest it deserves. Before looking to pills or quick fixes to get to sleep, take a holistic approach to your sleep habits to help you elevate your energy during waking hours.

SET YOUR SLEEP UP FOR SUCCESS
1. Motivate your melatonin production
Melatonin is a hormone produced by the pineal gland that helps our body recognize it's time to go to sleep. Exposure to light blocks this production. Therefore, making sure your bedroom is as dark as possible at night will help your body make melatonin. Dim the lights an hour or two before bed to prepare for sleep. Use blackout shades or curtains to keep your room as dark as possible.

If you're on your laptop in bed or scrolling on your phone waiting to feel tired, you're only making it harder to fall asleep. Power down at least an hour before bed and keep electronic devices away from your bed if possible.

2. Down regulate your nervous system

Your body wants to sleep. It has a built-in rhythm that is meant to naturally allow your body to sleep at night and be well rested and energized in the morning. But when we live our lives in a heightened state of stress and anxiety, we unknowingly fight against this rhythm. We keep our fight-or-flight response activated for most of the day and don't remember that we must take action to activate the parasympathetic nervous system, also known as rest and digest mode. There are many ways to do this depending on what feels good to you. Here are some suggestions:

- Breathe. Take long deep breaths in through the nose and out through the mouth. You can head back to the breathwork exercise in orange belt.
- Foam roll.
- Listen to a guided meditation.
- Listen to sleep music, ocean waves, forest, or rain sounds.
- Light a candle or burn some palo santo (just make sure you blow them out completely before falling asleep).
- Read a book. Keep it positive (like this one) and not a book that triggers any negative or stressful feelings.
- Keep a Gratitude Journal. List at least three things you are grateful for each day. You'll cultivate a feeling of abundance and peace by focusing on the good things in your life.

• Stretch all the muscles in your body where you tend to hold the most tension: neck, shoulders, lower back, hip flexors, hamstrings, or calves. A full body stretch can be delightful before bed.

Foods Fit for a Warrior

Nothing makes me sadder than clients who start obsessing over food, counting calories or using a points system. To them, food has become nothing more than a calculation. A bunch of numbers on their plate that must add up to the right amount or else they're in danger of disappointment from the scale. These systems do have their benefits and have helped many people realize the importance of energy consumption versus energy expenditure. However, food can be much more than something you must manipulate in order to control your weight.

Food can be enjoyable. Food can heal. Food is your friend. It's just been tainted for so many of us so it feels like the enemy. Something you need to restrict or regulate. A source of shame and guilt. Again, those feelings usually stem from childhood. Someone told you that you eat too much or commented on your weight in a negative way. Heck, I've even had clients who were forced to go to Weight Watchers meetings by their parents when they were young. Maybe a coach told you to lose weight to be competitive in your ballet class or on your rowing team. Or perhaps you were in an abusive family or relationship, and you used food as a source of comfort to soothe the pain. Of course, these experiences leave scars on the food/body relationship.

It's not lost on me that I was very lucky to grow up in an Italian American family in which food was abundant, healthy, and the source of so much joy. My father was deep into nutrition when I was a kid. No soda, no cereals with added sugar (this meant unfrosted Mini-Wheats!), and very little processed food were allowed in the house. I still ate junky food in moderation when I was with friends, or occasionally at home, but it wasn't readily available at my fingertips. We sat at the table together and had conversations as we ate healthy dinners that my mom cooked. I can't be more grateful for growing up with a healthy relationship to food. Especially now after working with so many clients that see food as their foe.

After fifteen years of coaching clients to healthier eating habits, I know for sure that the following guidelines are universal enough to create a better relationship with food for everyone.

1. **Eat whole foods.** Shop mostly from the perimeters of the grocery store where the fresh foods are kept.

2. **Eat mostly plant based.** You can't really go wrong when most of your food comes from vegetables, fruit, legumes, mushrooms, nuts, and seeds.

3. **Eat healthy fats.** The brain needs omega-3 fatty acids to use as building blocks for its cells, for hormone production, and to fight inflammation. Get them from mostly plant-based sources like avocado, nuts, and seeds or from wild-caught fish.

4. **Eat high-quality protein from plants and animals** (if you want). Organic legumes, nuts, and seeds. Pasture-raised eggs. Free-range meat. Wild-caught fish. If you can afford it, invest in the best quality protein you can get. If it comes

from an animal source, avoiding factory farmed animals will reduce your risk of eating meat contaminated with growth hormones and an overabundance of antibiotics. When animals are fed their natural diet, the fat on their bodies will be in a healthier ratio of anti-inflammatory fats.

5. **Cook with anti-inflammatory herbs and spices.** Add basil, cilantro, cinnamon, ginger, rosemary, turmeric, and other spices to not just boost the flavor of your meal but to enhance the anti-inflammatory effects of the meal.

Move That Butt!

Our bodies were made to move. They were not designed to sit in a chair and stare at a screen all day. Even if that is your reality, you don't have to change your job to fit more movement into your day.

What gets in most people's way of a consistent fitness routine is an all-or-nothing attitude. People think they need to be hard-core exercising every day for at least an hour in a gym to achieve a healthy, fit body. This couldn't be further from the truth. All-or-nothings usually start an intense workout challenge, often in January, and within weeks (or even days), they blow off their workout. One blown-off workout becomes two and then the Screw It attitude ensues. They go all in on the cupcakes at the office because . . . screw it, they missed their workout. They order greasy takeout because . . . screw it, they already ate cupcakes. They sleep through their alarm the next day because . . . screw it. They give up on themselves and revert to the same unhealthy habits that got them to where they were in the first place. Drained. Deflated. Defeated.

I start my clients out slowly when it comes to their exercise routines. In fact, I don't even like calling it exercise because many people have negative associations with that word. So we use movement. Move that ass. Every day. Just a little bit. Slowly, over time you start to experience small wins. A feeling of accomplishment. A little more room in your tight jeans. More energy throughout your day. Less stress. These small wins become motivators to keep going and possibly even increase the intensity, length, or frequency of your movement sessions.

How much should you move your body each day? It depends on what your baseline is. Are you starting from the couch? Then start with five minutes of walking per day. After a few weeks, add another five minutes either to the first five or break it up throughout the day and go for a second five-minute movement session later on.

Are you a fairly active person already? You get your kids off to school in the morning, commute to and from work, and get home to make dinner and do more chores? Great. Then carve out fifteen minutes of movement for yourself. The act of taking that time for you and your health is going to feel powerful. You deserve that time to invest in your peace and happiness.

Ideally your movement sessions should fall into three buckets:

1. **Cardio:** Get your heart rate up and break a sweat. Great for your heart and your spirit as you release happy chemicals called endorphins. This doesn't mean you have to do sprints or suffer through a spin class you hate. Walk, dance, jump rope, or take a boxing class. There are endless options.

2. **Strength:** Lift heavy things. You'll feel strong and powerful,

boost your resting metabolic rate (the rate that your body burns calories), and tone your body, which enhances your confidence.

3. **Flexibility and recovery:** Yoga, Pilates, foam rolling, and stretching. Any of these modalities will help your body stay flexible, prevent injury, and calm your mind so you can feel more at peace.

If you're a gym rat and love the effects of a sweaty workout session, then more power to you. But for those of you who dread the gym, there's hope for you too. Consistency is key to building your mind, body, and spirit energy slowly and sustainably. Just start!

Get Outside

We need the outdoors in our lives. We need sunshine and fresh air. We even need dirt to cultivate a healthy immune system. But we have become creatures of comfort. Staying indoors all summer in the air conditioning because it's too hot outside. Or staying indoors all winter long because it's cold. Depending on your location, I get that it can be tricky to get your nature fix, but making it a priority will have lasting mental and physical benefits.

Receiving beams of sunshine will boost vitamin D production in your body, which is essential for a functioning immune system, strong bones, and healthy brain function. Studies show that taking a "nature pill," the equivalent to connecting with nature for about twenty minutes, can significantly decrease cortisol levels.

So, go forest bathe. Hug a tree. Go for a hike. If you live in a city, head to the nearest park and sit on the grass. If you live near a lake or ocean, spend some time there. Find your "nature pill," and you will cultivate more peace and energy in your life.

Surround Yourself with Shiny Happy People

People who tend to complain about the littlest things get offended by everyone and everything, feel slighted by the universe, and feel the need to talk about it all constantly . . . are robbing you of your energy. When I'm around these energy vampires, I feel compelled to keep my distance. But I didn't always feel that way. I sometimes would get sucked into the negativity too. Or at times, I would try to force them to reframe their circumstance to see the positive. Now I know that just like garlic repels a vampire, I can create my own ways of dealing with them.

We learned in orange belt that if our boundaries are being crossed, we have two ways to deal with it: create distance or communicate our boundaries. The same goes for your negative colleagues, family, or friends. Sometimes it's not possible to cut these people out of your lives completely, but you can create space from them. Don't allow yourself to get sucked into their downward spiral of negativity. Stay above it. Change the conversation. Smile and nod while you say positive affirmations to yourself. Shift your body language to a resourceful and confident state. Move yourself physically away from the conversation. Do whatever you need to do to protect yourself from the energy drain.

Most importantly, actively seek out positive people and cultivate more energy-gaining relationships in your life. Is there someone at your office who is always smiling, always has something nice to say, and genuinely feels good to be around? Hang around that person more. Date, cohabitate, and marry positive people. Work out in a positive vibe gym or find your happy tribe of yoga people. Find people who have similar interests to you who are on a path to more peace, power, and purpose.

Play Like a Pro

Finally, playtime shouldn't stop after childhood. Research shows that play releases endorphins, improves brain functionality, and enhances creativity. Too many women don't make time for play because "adulting" has taken over their lives. Work all day, get home to take care of the kids, do chores, or work more. Pass out and hit repeat the next day. The weekend comes and you fill it with a to-do list of personal chores like laundry, or you plant yourself on the couch for a Netflix binge because you're just too tired to deal.

My favorite playtime as a kid was to be outside on my bicycle for hours at a time. I was allowed to roam the neighborhood until sundown. I felt free and happy. My husband and I now make it a point to go out and cycle around town a few times each week. Sometimes it's to cruise down to the beach or to head to the local wine bar for a date night. It works every time to help us feel happy and free, just like we did as kids. In my view, it's essential that we all take time regularly to connect with those kinds of feelings, to do stuff just because it makes us smile. It's one of the best ways to recharge and connect with ourselves. So what makes you feel playful?

Exercise: Playtime!

Some of us are so removed from our playful selves that we've forgotten what kinds of activities we used to enjoy. This exercise will help you create a menu of activities that light you up and make you feel like a playful kid again. Whether you were an outgoing kid who loved to play with friends or more introverted and coveted time alone dressing up your dolls, allowing yourself to rediscover that joy you felt as a kid will reconnect you with your soul so you can feel more peaceful and purposeful.

1. Let's take a trip down memory lane. Find memories of your younger self at playtime. Think back to memories from early childhood and ones from your teenage years. What activities made you feel most alive? Most fun? Most happy?

2. Write them down in your journal and circle the activities that still sound like fun to you now. Even if they may seem weird or a waste of time today, I promise you that there is probably an adult version of that activity that would make your heart sing.

3. Look for ways to bring some of that fun back today. Did you like to draw as a kid? Trade in the crayons (or not!) for a watercolor class or an adult coloring book. Did you love to bake in your Easy-Bake Oven? Start baking again or go take a pastry class at the nearest culinary school. Were you a master of Monopoly or Trivial Pursuit? Get your friends over once a month for game night. Carve out time for your creative, playful, younger self and have more fun. You 1,000 percent deserve it, and your energy will soar!

Belt Test: Blue to Red (#badassbelttest)

Are you ready to elevate your energy and get a taste of what life can feel like with more vitality? This blue belt test will challenge you to practice radical self-care. It will guide you to design a day for yourself that encompasses all the lessons from this chapter. If necessary, you can spread this out over two days if you're pressed for time, but make sure to complete all the exercises to pass your test!

START YOUR TEST

Right now, all you will do is plan out the day (or days) that you will complete the test. Grab your journal and pen and complete the following prompts.

- I will complete the following blue to red belt test on _____ (date).
- I will drink half my body weight in ounces of water: ½ body weight (pounds) = _____ ounces.
- I will attempt to get a full night's sleep the night before and the night of my test. In order for that to happen, I'll need to prepare by (head back to the Sleep Like a Star section for ideas):
- I will eat three delicious meals that include foods fit for a warrior. The menus I'm planning are
  - Breakfast:
  - Lunch:
  - Dinner:

- Shopping list:
- I will move my ass and fit in a movement session of
  _____ (type of movement) for _____ (length
  of time).
- I will get myself outdoors and take a nature pill. Here's
  where I'll go: _____.
- I always feel more positive after hanging out with
  _____ (name up to five people in your life). I'm
  going to reach out to one or more of them and set up a
  phone call, Zoom meeting, or in-person chat and discuss

  _____.

- I will incorporate playtime by choosing an activity from
  the Playtime! section and do it. I choose: _____.

Now go make it happen! Once you have completed your day
of radical self-care, congratulations! You have passed your belt
test and now have the tools to elevate your energy for a lifetime
and not just a day. 🏯

CHAPTER SIX

Red Belt: Connect with Your Warrior Within

I've already told you the story of being completely blindsided by the ex-boyfriend who had a baby with someone else. What I haven't said is that there were plenty of signs throughout the years that would have had many people running for the hills. Like how I questioned the woman's name that came up on caller ID when he called my cell phone. He explained it away as someone who helped him get a great deal on his cell phone plan. Or the time I organized a birthday party for him, and this random woman showed up whom I'd never met before. Or when I saw the Active Labor playlist on his iPod and thought it was music for doing physical labor when in reality it was a list of songs to play for the woman giving birth to his child. And if I'm really honest with myself, the gut feeling I had all along was that this man had some deep, dark secrets, darker than I really wanted to know. These little naggings were there all along, and I either dismissed them or allowed myself to be gaslighted out of investigating them further.

Those nagging feelings were the voice of my inner warrior. The voice that I've learned over the years to lean into and trust. However, the younger version of me ignored her and buried her head in the sand. On some level, I didn't want to find out what he was up to. Instead of letting my younger self and the decisions she made infuriate me, I now send her compassion. Because of her, I will honor my intuition going forward. I'll tune in to my inner warrior when she speaks to me and ask her questions when I don't fully understand the message. I'll investigate. I'll recalibrate. I'll earn her trust back slowly each time I lean into the message.

We've all heard a voice within, had a gut feeling, or felt an inner knowing. On the path to becoming a black belt, you'll become more aware of this inner guidance, and you'll learn to trust it and yourself more than ever. This intuition can do more than save you from danger and bad relationships; it can help you create your unique journey of life. It will help pull you toward the experiences most meaningful to you and away from people, places, and things that no longer serve you. You'll be able to make better choices about your career, friends, and partners. You'll become more creative and have more ease around problem-solving. When you go within and connect with your inner warrior, you will find more peace, which will help guide you toward your purpose.

What It Means to Be a Red Belt

Red belts in martial arts prepare for their black belt by deepening their inward training. Meditation, breathwork, and a focus on slower forms of movement become a bigger part of their practice. They begin to see the benefits, not just on the mat, but spilling out into other parts of their lives. They begin to connect with their inner warrior.

On the mat, the martial artist will enhance her sparring skills as she gets focused. She's able to pick up on her opponent's telegraphing of their next moves by paying attention to small, detailed movements in their hips and shoulders. She knows if they are about to throw a roundhouse kick or a hook punch before it actually occurs. It's as if time slows down and she can spot danger and avoid it before it takes her down. Being in this zone helps her make decisions on the fly because she knows hesitation and self-doubt will put her in harm's way. Her enhanced awareness and deeper connection to her spirit help her read situations. She's more grounded and more efficient in her actions, and she trusts her inner voice. She is more at peace and is realizing how powerful she is.

My goal for you through red belt level is to help you slow down to become more present. Once you're more present, you will heighten your awareness. Once you're more aware, you will gain more access to the inner guidance your warrior within provides. You'll feel the tugging toward people, places, and experiences that fill you with more joy. You'll be able to feel the repulsion from the people, places, and experiences that drag you down. The more you listen, the more you can hear. And life will start to feel like you're flowing with it instead of fighting an uphill battle.

When you're connected with your inner warrior, you'll start to see your relationships deepen, your career will advance, and your health will flourish. You'll feel a deeper sense of peace from within, which makes you unshakeable and a powerful force in this world.

At blue belt level we realized we need to practice radical self-care to avoid burnout and elevate our energy. Now we're kicking it down a notch. We're going even deeper. Within. To connect with the OG version of you, the you that knows your true potential. You may call her your soul, your spirit, or your highest self. I refer to her as your inner warrior.

Your inner warrior stays steady in the face of adversity. She can feel fear and act anyway. Your inner warrior is unshakeable, wise, and always wants the best outcome for you. She's always there for you even when life feels like a battle. Your inner warrior will whisper to you and send you messages guiding you toward the next right step when you're faced with challenges. Connecting with your inner warrior is like going home where there's always comfort waiting for you. You just need to slow down and go within to find her.

Slow Down to Speed Up

There have been many times in my life when I felt like I was just racing to get to the next goal, whether that was a financial milestone or booking a certain number of speaking gigs throughout the year. I'd be so focused on the doing that I often forgot to slow down and be present to how I was being. I'd be focused on the next big thing without appreciating the present moment.

I felt happiness but that happiness was usually dependent on an outside circumstance, like getting a new client or celebrating a special occasion with family or friends. In general, I had an underlying sense of worry. Worry that I couldn't get done what I needed to. Worry that I couldn't reach my goals. Worry about money. Worry about family. Worry that everyone was passing me by, and I couldn't catch up. That worry robbed me of peace, and I'm sure that trickled into decisions I made in my personal and professional life. I acted from a place of scarcity and lack versus trust and faith in myself. Thankfully, that all changed when I made slowing down and connecting with my inner warrior a daily practice.

Early on as a martial artist, I learned different meditation techniques: sitting meditations, breathing meditations, walking meditations, and moving meditations. I enjoyed them all when I was forced to do them in class, but I rarely took my meditation with me outside the dojo. I pretended I didn't have time for it. What I didn't realize was that meditation and mindfulness free up more time in your life as you become more focused and intentional. I didn't realize the profound benefits meditation could have on my life and on my way of being.

It wasn't until I attended an intuition training in Los Angeles taught by Vishen Lakhiani, founder of the personal development education platform Mindvalley, that I fully committed to a daily meditation practice. After four years of daily meditation, I can say that it has, hands down, changed my life for the better. The change in me is not easy to pinpoint. Unlike in the blue belt chapter where simple changes in food or movement can change your appearance, a meditation practice may not be visible to an outsider. The change is deep within.

I feel more at peace. I'm calmer and less reactive. I feel more confident in my abilities and more at ease when taking risks. I worry less and have more faith that things will work out. I'm more inspired to live out my purpose. They are subtle changes with profound effects, all from a consistent mindfulness practice. Imagine your life with similar tweaks. Would you feel any different about your life and how you want to live it? What would you be able to accomplish? How would you allow yourself to feel?

For me, it took a daily, dedicated meditation practice to slow down and become more present. Yet, there are many ways to reach the same destination, to connect with your inner warrior. For many of us, the first step is to recognize how fast we're going in the first place. If you're spinning on a hamster wheel and feel like life is running you versus you're running your life, it's time to reassess. If you can barely squeeze in time to read this book, if you don't have time to pursue your hobbies and your dreams, it's time to slow down and tune in.

When we run ourselves ragged, it's difficult to hear our inner warrior guiding us toward happiness and away from power-draining people, places, and things. When we're going too fast, we're usually run-down and headed for burnout. We get sloppy and we make mistakes, costing us time and energy. We ignore signals that are guiding us to safety and higher purpose. We're more reactive in our lives, which robs us of peace. Do you find yourself snapping at your kids or your partner? Do you feel like your fuse is short with your colleagues or friends? Maybe you don't just need a vacation (even though I'm sure that wouldn't be a bad thing!), maybe you just need to slow down and commit to a mindfulness practice.

Short fuses are a symptom of not having enough space between a stimulus and your reaction. A stimulus can be someone accidentally spilling coffee on your favorite new pair of jeans, and the reaction would be how you deal with it. A short-fused person may get angry and react by yelling or cursing the person out. Someone else may pause before they react. They'll put some space in between the stimulus and the response and have more control of how they want to respond. Perhaps the person who made the mistake will have time to apologize in a sincere way, which diffuses the situation even more. Imagine having more of a gap in reaction time with people you care about. How would your relationships change if you were more at peace?

As you can see, slowing down gives you more control over your moods and how you react to other people and circumstances. Once that happens, you'll find yourself becoming more efficient with your words and actions. When we become more efficient, we save time and energy and therefore have more opportunity to use that time for our hobbies or dreams.

We know that practices like meditation help us combat stress, help us sleep better, and can even lower blood pressure. But something you won't read in a scientific study is that mindfulness practices also help you feel more confident. I've never felt more badass in my life than after a deep meditation session. Even when I was training as a black belt in hapkido, sparring, or breaking boards on fire, I didn't feel as confident as I do now with my connection to my inner warrior. That's because when you're in control of your emotions and how you react, when you're more intentional with your words and actions, you feel like you're the one in the driver's seat of your life. You're willing to take more risks, because even if you fail, you know you won't let yourself become an emotional wreck because of it. You know that even when life gets really challenging, you can just go back "home" to connect with your inner warrior where you can find peace and guidance.

If you're like I was when I thought I didn't have time to slow down, that's okay. You can ease into your red belt lesson by taking baby steps. You can experiment with different practices to slow down, like meditation, yoga, breathwork, or journaling. There is one method that I highly recommend, which is easy to do and works almost immediately: a gratitude practice.

When we express gratitude, the brain releases dopamine and serotonin, the same feel-good chemicals that we get from eating sugar. A regular gratitude practice has been shown to decrease cortisol levels and therefore help with stress regulation. Essentially, we can swap the cookie binge for a gratitude practice and get longer-lasting positive effects minus the sugar crash and mood swings.

Each morning I connect with my inner warrior, and I start the process by bringing to mind things I'm grateful for. Even on my worst days, I can always recall at least a few things in my life in that moment that will bring a smile to my face and a warm feeling to my heart.

The easiest way for me to get there is to start with my cats, Fig and Olive. I picture them, and sometimes one of them may even crawl into my lap, making it even easier to feel the calm feeling of thankfulness. I'll visualize sipping on my favorite Nespresso coffee that I'll make when my meditation is complete. I'll think of my husband, my family, and my friends. I'll give thanks for the home I get to live in and the ability to live in a city as beautiful as Santa Monica. My heartbeat slows and a smile spontaneously appears. And that's just the beginning of my meditation.

By doing this, I'm consciously choosing how I want my day to begin versus reacting to the life stuff being thrown my way. The rejection e-mails in my inbox, the bills, the cat vomit on the carpet, the negative news alerts on my phone, or the social media posts I'm "supposed to" be posting. I come first. I've even trained the cats to wait patiently for their breakfast until my meditation is finished. It's as if they intuitively know that I'm up to something important because they (usually) sit quietly and wait close by for their kibble.

When you make this time for yourself in the beginning of your day, you're saying to your inner warrior that your well-being is your highest priority. That in order to be the best version of yourself at home and at work, you need to take this time to cultivate your presence and set your state for the day. You get to take your power back from the bills, the news, and the pressures at work by choosing how you want to feel. Not letting negative feelings run your day. Feeling grateful for even the little things in your life can instantly have you go from a day filled with dread and reactivity to a day of hope and intentional action.

The Two Minutes of Gratitude Exercise

1. Take out your journal and write Gratitude List at the top of a clean page.
2. Set a timer for one minute.
3. List all the people, places, things, or experiences you can think of that you are grateful for.
4. Once the minute is up, set your timer for one more minute.
5. Look at the list and review each entry. Feel the feelings of gratitude as you think of each item as a true gift in your life.

Notice how quickly you can change how you feel just by con-centrating on gratitude. Use this exercise as often as you'd like. It's especially powerful in the mornings to set your state and in the evenings as you wind down for bed, particularly if you tend to feel anxious before you snooze. Also, your thoughts are portable and powerful enough if you don't have pen and paper handy.

Listen with Your Whole Body

Now that you have a practice to become more present, the next step is to go even deeper to enhance your awareness. One of the first lessons I teach in my self-defense trainings is about deepening your awareness of your surroundings. Scanning for red flags by being fully present. That means cell phones are put away and earbuds are out. Eyes and ears are open and taking in information about people, places, and activity around you. When we intentionally practice this, we allow our intuition to guide us to avoid danger and stay safe. On top of that, greater awareness can deepen our relationships and guide us toward more of what we want.

To build that awareness, learn to listen with your whole body. We start with our ears because most of us associate listening with our ears. Yet, how many of us have really mastered that? I grew up in a large, extended family where it's hard to get a word in edgewise at any family gathering. Everyone talks at one another all at once, and usually the loudest person wins. That doesn't leave room for a whole lot of listening. After becoming present to it, I realized this is not something I want to emulate in my communication style.

During my career journey of being a health coach, I had to, and still must work on, becoming an active listener. Active listening is a technique in which you carefully listen to a person's verbal and nonverbal communication. That means you're actively hearing what they are saying and noticing what their body language is portraying. You can then paraphrase what someone said and repeat it back to them to make sure you understood their message. In difficult situations and relationships where communication is strained, this can be an extremely helpful technique.

When we practice active listening, we gather more information, and information is power. Also, the people on the receiving end feel heard and seen. Hence, your relationships can transform because they appreciate your company. Remember to strike a balance between active listening and contributing to the conversation as well. I've been in situations where I've practiced my active listening so well that the other person never stopped talking! And when I leave situations like that, I tend to feel a bit drained. Visualizing a nice ping-pong game of communication is a great way to listen, connect, and be heard at the same time.

Once we can listen better with our ears, we can start to work on gathering more information with our eyes. Watching people's body language will give you a better understanding of what that person is feeling while they're speaking. Tuning in to nonverbal cues can tell you if someone is engaged in your story or checking their watch because they're waiting for you to stop talking. You may be able to detect if someone is sad, stressed, or happy by their facial expressions. You may sense someone's insecurities by the way they hold their body when they're speaking to you. Listening with our eyes is helpful from the street to the boardroom.

If you can listen with both your ears and your eyes, the next level of listening is with your body. Can you feel another person's energy? Can you sense when there's tension in a room or when someone is generally excited to meet you? This is the deepest level of listening, when you can hear someone without them opening their mouth to speak. This is when you can hear what is not being said. When you can sense if someone's intentions are genuine or not. This is the type of listening that will have you stand out as a badass leader in your work, with your family, and in your community.

In everyday life, listening in this way can mean sensing your boss or employee is struggling to stay motivated. You can then connect with them and ask if they're okay. Boom. You've just made a connection with someone who may not have otherwise confided in you. If you can tell when your partner is feeling disconnected, you can dig in and see if there's a way they could use your support. Boom. You just deepened your relationship. If you can sense when a business deal just doesn't feel right, or that the person or company you're about to partner with doesn't have your best intentions in mind, you can pull out of the deal. Boom. You just saved yourself money and headaches. If you can sense that a guy you're dating isn't forthcoming with details of his life, and something feels shady about him, you can choose to find out if he's worthy of your time. Boom. You get back all that energy you wasted on wondering if he's really that into you. Or, God forbid, you sense that someone is about to commit an act of violence and you can get away or fight back. Boom. You may have just saved your life.

Exercise: Master the Art of Listening

The intention of this exercise is to practice listening on all three levels so you can deepen your awareness.

1. During your next conversation with your partner, colleague, client, boss, friend, or family member, listen more

than you speak. Even if you're used to carrying the conversation or talking more than the other person, shut your lips when you have the urge to jump in and talk.

2. Practice active listening by hearing what they are saying and repeating it back to them. You can start with a phrase like, "So what I hear you saying is . . . {fill in the blank}." Then you can follow up with, "Is that right?"

3. Listen with your eyes. Take in their body language and see what comes to mind. Do they seem tense or relaxed? Do they make eye contact with you or dart their eyes around the room? Do they fidget or are they still? Simply observe.

4. Listen with your body. How does what they're saying (or not saying) feel to you?

5. After the conversation is complete, check in with yourself and see what you learned from that experience. Did it shift the conversation, or the energy between the two of you, or your relationship in any way? Did you hear something that you couldn't have heard if you were busy talking?

The more we practice the art of listening, the more it raises our awareness and gives our inner warrior the opportunity to communicate with us. Some people will hear an actual message, some may see an image or a mental movie play out, and many of us just feel these messages in our gut.

Listen to Your Intuition

In his book, *The Gift of Fear,* safety and security expert Gavin de Becker writes, "Intuition is the journey from A to Z without stopping at any other letter along the way. It is knowing without knowing why." It's like having an inner GPS that is always guiding you whether you're conscious of it or not. *Head straight in this direction. Now turn right. Trust this person. Do NOT trust this person. Don't take the job. Start the side hustle.* All with the intent of keeping you safe and guiding you toward happiness.

Intuitive thoughts seem to come out of nowhere at times, yet they're usually given to us by our subconscious mind, which has the ability to come to conclusions faster than our conscious mind can, according to de Becker.

When we're in the middle of a challenge, many of us look to outside sources for answers. I know tons of women who pay boat-loads of money to a psychic to tell them their future, but won't listen to the signals and messages they receive daily from their own intuition. Maybe it's because they're unconsciously blocking the whispers with their fast-paced lives and never-ending to-do lists. Maybe we do hear the whispers and choose to ignore them. Or maybe we hear the messages but don't trust ourselves enough to take action on them. We think we're just being paranoid or overly cautious. We defy our intuition and sometimes put ourselves in harm's way even when our intuition is telling us to run like hell.

I can tell when I'm not listening to my inner warrior these days. I start to feel out of alignment. Wobbly. Off purpose. When I'm there I've realized that I'm not listening because of fear. I'm either fearful of repeating a past mistake, or I'm afraid of failing at something in the future. Either way, I can't allow fear to run my life. In those times, I double down on my meditation practice, become present, and realign.

When you listen to your intuition, whether the outcome is positive or not, it is an empowering experience in learning to trust yourself. When you trust your inner warrior, the confidence within you shines outwardly, busting straight through your heart. The power within you slays your self-doubt, leaving you grounded and steady.

A Detective Mindset

The more information you gather, the stronger your intuition muscle becomes. When my father was young, he joined the NYPD and worked his way up to becoming a detective. He retired shortly after I was born to pursue a new career in real estate, but his detective mindset never left him. Growing up with a retired detective as my dad wasn't always fun. I knew I couldn't get away with too much sneaking around, and he would grill any boy that called the house phone. He even asked for their last names and made them spell it! But later in life I recognized the perks. When I moved into my first dorm room at my college in the Bronx, Dad was with me on moving day. He checked the building's entrances and exits, communal rooms and windows, fire escapes, and the locks on my door. Post-college, while living in Manhattan, any time I moved apartments, Dad was there to investigate my safety.

His detective mindset strengthened his intuition muscle through two main practices: observing and asking questions. By adopting a detective mindset, you too can become even better at avoiding problems before they occur and making decisions that support your well-being.

Observing helps you enhance your awareness by listening with your whole being, which we just covered in the previous section. Asking questions deepens your connection to your inner warrior even further. We can ask questions outwardly to others (like in the clarifying questions block from the orange belt chapter) and inwardly to ourselves to get clarification on the gut feelings and hunches we have. The next time you have a gut feeling, a hunch, or a nagging and you're not clear on the message or you're not sure on the next step to take, quiet down and connect. Then ask yourself questions like:

- What is this message trying to tell me?
- What else should I know about this situation?
- What's the next right action to take?

Be as specific in your questions as possible, and wait for answers. They may not come to you in the moment, but they may show up when you're washing your hair or taking a walk. Trust that these messages have your back and want the best for you even when the answers seem hard and uncomfortable.

"Difficulties come when you don't pay attention to life's whisper. Life always whispers to you first, but if you ignore the whisper, sooner or later you'll get a scream."

—**Oprah Winfrey**

Strengthening the Intuition Muscle

Taking action on your intuition is how you build back your self-trust. Being able to hear the messages is great, but if you do nothing about them, that's when you beat yourself up. We get pissed at ourselves for not acting when we knew we should or could have. I know that in many instances, following your intuition can be scary as heck, especially when it's a big decision like quitting your job or leaving a relationship. If that's the case, then start with baby steps. Instead of handing in your resignation tomorrow, start by reaching out to a recruiter or researching how to start your own business. Instead of packing your bags and leaving your marriage, reach out to a friend or therapist for support on making a plan.

After two decades of teaching self-defense, I've heard countless stories from women who acted on their intuition, and it saved their life. I know women who have been able to get out of abusive relationships before they got physically violent. I know women who have been physically threatened and avoided an altercation by spontaneously acting in a way that got them out of the situation. I even know women whose intuition helped them fight back just enough for the predator to change their mind.

Intuition can not only keep you from physical harm, it can also help deepen your connection to your body and guide you to better health and well-being. So many of us dismiss aches, markings, or unexplained behaviors in our body as normal because we're too busy to investigate the cause. We push through the discomfort of things like unexplained weight loss, severe period pain, migraines, and rashes, secretly hoping they'll magically go away. Not to mention when we do head to our doctor's office with vague symptoms, we're sometimes dismissed by professionals or given a pill to cover the symptoms up, only for the issue to persist. It's a drag to have to deal with health issues. It takes time and energy to slow down and investigate them, but sometimes your life depends on it.

Rosie grew up in Israel spending a lot of time in the sunshine without SPF. She moved to the United States as a young adult and started getting regular skin checks by a dermatologist. She was twenty-five when she noticed one mole that didn't look like the others. It was darker in color and something about it just didn't feel right. She went to her dermatologist who dismissed it as normal. Still, Rosie had a nagging feeling about it. She finally went for a second opinion, and her new doctor found she had an aggressive melanoma growing on her skin. His words still haunt her to this day: "If we didn't find this when we did, you wouldn't have made it another two years." Rosie listened to her intuition and it saved her life.

Instead of ignoring the odd-shaped mole, the pain, or unexplained fatigue, what if we start to consider every weird symptom as a messenger that contains wisdom that leads us to better health? Perhaps then we would take the time to slow down, ask more questions, and find the resources, people, and answers we need to take the next right step.

Enter the Flow Zone

I'm sure you've been there before. A time in your life when everything flowed effortlessly. You moved through work or a relationship without struggle or hustle. Coincidences occurred more often, and life seemed to be on your side. The right people showed up. The solutions to your problems appeared almost magically. You felt deep happiness in your soul.

I remember first feeling this during my hapkido training. After a few years of devoted practice, I began entering the Flow Zone when I rehearsed my forms or *katas* (the Japanese word for "form" or a choreographed sequence of martial arts movements). It didn't happen every day, only when I felt most relaxed, rested, and ready. One move flowed into the next. The only noise I'd hear was the sharp snap of my uniform as I threw the perfect punch. My breath was in tune with my movements: exhaling on the effort, inhaling on the ease. Everything else was tuned out.

Now I'm able to bring this zone off the mat and into my life.

I feel myself tapping into it the most when I'm speaking onstage, and it helps me connect with my audience. I've given hundreds of talks at this point so there's a more relaxed energy that flows through my words. My intuition guides me to tell certain stories or to make certain gestures or jokes. There's an ease that feels like magic, when in reality, I know it's because I have practiced this over and over again, both live in front of audiences and in my head through visualization.

When you're feeling stuck, it's especially hard to imagine entering the Flow Zone. Life might feel more like you're moving through quicksand, and, no matter what you do, things aren't working the way you want them to. That's okay. The key to snapping yourself out of those funks and mastering your performance is consistency and visualization.

Whatever you're working toward, you can adopt habituation to make entering the Flow Zone a more regular and accessible part of your life. Whether you're trying to enter the zone during athletic training or as you sit down to write your book, getting serious about setting up a daily practice is key. So many people give up on their goals because they don't see results right away, or because the task at hand is too daunting. But chunking it down and showing up "to the mat" every day helps set your mind and body up for success.

In the beginning of my meditation practice, I never felt like I was "doing it right," because it always seemed too difficult to concentrate. When I finally committed and showed up every single morning for months at a time, I began to experience the benefits I shared in the beginning of the chapter. I felt like I was going deeper within, and it became easier to access that state over time.

Writing this book felt like a daunting task when I first began. I was sporadic with my writing schedule and I felt like I was forcing words onto the page. Once I started showing up to the page on a regular basis, the practice of it helped me tap into my creative source. The habituation of showing up to your mat is what eventually gets you unstuck. Patience and perseverance are your two best friends when you want to feel the flow.

Visualization is the cherry on top. Visualization will take you from good to great at whatever you're up to in life. Seeing something happen before it happens plants the seed in your mind that will help pull you toward making something happen. Again, it's not magic. You don't just close your eyes, visualize, and your goals appear. But setting the intention and seeing it happen help keep you focused on the direction you want to move toward and guide you toward the next right step.

If athletes can visualize themselves winning their competitions, so too can we visualize acing our tests, winning over the client, solving a problem, or attracting our soul mate. Visualization can help you tap into your inner warrior to guide you to your next right step, and doing it regularly will allow you to enter the Flow Zone more often.

Belt Test: Red to Black (#badassbelttest)

How exciting! You have arrived at your black belt test. The final step to fully unleashing your badassery into the world. This test will challenge you to get on your mat and put to work all the concepts we covered in this chapter. In order to pass your test, you need only to complete this one time. However, to embody the lessons of the red belt, I highly encourage you to make this a daily practice. It will transform you and your life for the better. Subtly. Over time. Yet with profound effects.

PREPARE YOURSELF

1. Create your sacred space for your test, just as you have for each previous belt test. Removing yourself from as much outward noise as possible will be particularly helpful for this test.

START YOUR TEST

1. Sit upright or lie comfortably. Get in a comfortable position and close your eyes.

2. Set a timer. If you are a beginner, start with five minutes. If you already have a meditation practice, feel free to increase the time for this exercise.

3. Use deep belly breathing to relax your mind and body. You can use the 4x4x4 method from the orange belt chapter.

4. Once you feel relaxed, bring to mind at least five things you are grateful for. Be sure to sit with each thing long enough to feel the feelings of gratitude fill up your spirit.

5. Bring to mind an issue, challenge, or project you could use guidance or clarity on.

   Ask your inner warrior questions about this situation. You can ask things like, "What do I need to know about X?" "What can I learn from Y?" "What's the next right step to take?"

6. After each question, pause and listen for answers. Acknowledge how your inner warrior speaks to you. You may see an

image flash before your eyes or a mental movie playing out. You may hear a voice or sense a feeling.

7. Trusting your gut is essential to growing your intuitive muscle. If you receive clear messages from your intuition, act on them. Even small steps, like connecting with an old friend, help you build trust in your inner wisdom.

8. Now visualize the ideal outcome you'd like to create from the situation at hand. You don't have to know how you got there, just see yourself as if it's happened.

Congratulations, dear warrior. You are now a black belt of badassery! 🏯

CHAPTER SEVEN

Black Belt: Take the Lead

I n 2004, I took my test to become a black belt. The buildup was intense and the result was nothing short of transforma- tive. The test began at 4:00 A.M. After a fitful sleep, I got out of bed around 3:00 A.M. and walked the few blocks over to the dojo in the dark. When I entered the dojo, the mood was set. It was solemn, with dimmed lights and loud drumming music. Nobody spoke. We were quiet and focused as we stretched and warmed up. I didn't know what to expect, because the black belts that came before us never spoke about their black belt tests. Kind of like fight club. The rule is, you don't talk about fight club. I was nervous with an underlying twinge of excitement for what was to come. The transformation to black belt.

The test lasted for many hours. Maybe eight? It's all a blur now, but I remember at some point in the morning the sunshine entered the massive windows that lined the dojo. I remember being invited to a post-test celebratory dim sum brunch in the neighborhood at around noon, but I was too exhausted to go. In between, I mostly remember grueling hours of kicking, punching, sparring, rolling, and defending against every attack imaginable, and using my inner dialogue to guide me through the most challenging parts. The times where my arms felt like lead from all the push-ups, and my legs would quiver from holding stances so long. When my body felt like it had no more fuel, and it wanted to quit, I remember saying to myself, "I am not my body. I am not my mind." Over and over again. "I am not my body. I am not my mind." It wasn't a mantra I planned on using; it spontaneously came to me in the middle of the test because of my fight not to quit. It reminded me that I am so much greater than my quivering legs and my thoughts telling me to give up. It reaffirmed that my spirit is greater and far more powerful than my mind and body combined and can lead me through the hardest times and guide me toward more purpose.

Weeks after the test, we received our black belts. Never had I experienced a greater feeling of satisfaction. Not because of the brutal eightish-hour test, but from the years of training, discipline, and commitment before it. Every time I tied that belt around my waist, I was reminded of this. No matter what else was happening in my life, that belt reminded me of my strength and commitment to leveling up my mind, body, and spirit and my devotion to becoming a better human and a leader in my martial arts community. Soon, it was evident the effects of becoming a black belt in hapkido were spreading into all areas of my life. I taught more classes. I grew my own business as a personal trainer and health coach. I dove into personal development and attended dozens of seminars to better myself. I had more confidence to chase my dreams of becoming a coach, a public speaker, and an author with the mission of helping women feel more strong, safe, and powerful from the streets to the boardroom.

This is the way of the black belt. Taking control of your life. Leading. Giving back. Fighting for yourself, others, and a better world that we all deserve to live in.

What It Means to Be a Black Belt

Not everyone achieves their black belt in martial arts. In fact, most people quit long before because the commitment becomes too challenging. For those who do test for their black belt, there are requirements they must fill before even being considered as a candidate. In the dojo where I was trained, you must have dedicated at least one hundred hours to teaching others. And no, we weren't paid. You may consider it free labor, but the compensation for the giveback didn't have a monetary value. Martial arts wisdom goes deeper than that. Martial artists believe you cannot truly embody or master your skills without teaching them and passing them on for the good of others. You can't be a true leader without giving back.

Many martial artists begin their journey as white belts to learn self-defense or to get into shape, but along the way, they realize their training serves a higher purpose. They take on a leadership role in the dojo and feel fulfilled by watching their students' progress through the ranks. They realize becoming a black belt is truly an honor and that every drop of blood, sweat, or tears shed has been an integral part of their journey.

In life, becoming a black belt is about taking on a leadership role in your life and community and knowing what you stand for. You realize you were put here to serve a higher purpose. Your stress and anxiety diminish because you're less focused on your problems and more focused on your impact on others. You realize there are so many people who could use your unique talents and that by NOT giving them to the world you'd be depriving it of your gifts. You know that black belt level is not the end of your transformation. It's only the beginning and you are always a fabulous work in progress. You will leave this world just a little bit brighter because you were here.

Congratulations if you've made it this far! Like I said, most people give up on their personal development journey before reaching this stage. But you're still here! You have not given up on yourself. If you're feeling like you're at max capacity in your life or like you have no more left to give, hang in there. This is where you'll need to dig deep as you're right at the precipice of something awesome. The black belt version of you that you've been waiting for. You may even be surprised you're already practicing the way of the black belt. Wherever you are on your journey right now, I promise that soon, once you choose to become the leader of your life, your mojo will overfloweth.

Take the Lead

When I was younger and heard the word *leadership,* I automatically pictured men in gray pinstripe suits with gray hair sitting around large glass tables in a colorless boardroom. It felt like a concept that was reserved for people who followed a corporate or political career. It didn't feel like it was accessible to someone like me who was dressed in Lululemon workout clothes and went to work in people's homes to help them get more fit. It wasn't until I was climbing the ranks of my martial arts journey that I started to understand that I too could be a leader. At first in the microcosm of the dojo, and later in my personal and professional life as well.

What became clearer as the years went on is that being a leader is a choice we get to make. Nobody is coming to rescue us or secretly anoint us as a leader in our work, in our home, or in our communities. Nobody is going to save us from a case of the blahs or a life of unfulfillment. I realized that, if I wanted to be a leader, I needed to step up and take the lead by taking on and demonstrating the characteristics of a true leader. The kind of leader I admired and wanted to emulate.

As the years go on and my career and life are constantly changing and growing, I'm defining and redefining what kind of leader I want to be. You can do the same. Yet, there are some characteristics of black belt leadership that I am always striving to prioritize.

- Black belt leaders take a stand for others and causes greater than themselves.
- Black belt leaders find purpose in contribution.
- Black belt leaders are authentic and take responsibility for their words and actions.
- Black belt leaders help others rise.

No matter your gender, age, or profession, you can choose a life of leadership and true badassery. Your style of leadership will be unique to you. Your brand will be your own. But I know that if you stick to the black belt principles laid out in this chapter, you will rise above the noise. You will stand out for your bravery, and you will feel more badass with every passing day and with every passing year.

Take a Stand

My martial arts teacher always said, "If you don't stand for something, you'll fall for everything." In our individualist society today, it can be hard for people to step outside themselves to stand for a cause greater than themselves. It's the "American Way" to want to get ahead while focused on yourself and your immediate family. It's easy to ignore the bigger picture of connectedness and togetherness when life feels like a rat race to the top. When you're saddled with student loan debt and the thought of buying a house feels unattainable, it's easy to play it safe and do your best to climb the corporate ladder rung by rung without thinking of community.

Many of us might also be scared to take a stand for causes out of fear of criticism or backlash. We witnessed this during the #MeToo movement when women who shared their stories of sexual assault were dismissed, discredited, and even put on the stand to plead their case. Currently, we see people taking a stand for racial equality who are called performative, radical, and dangerous and even receive death threats for condemning racism. Even in the wellness world it's rare that the advice from your favorite influencer is guiding you toward community care over self-care.

When you're clear about what you stand for, you become unshakeable. Before I knew what I stood for, I would cringe at the thought of someone criticizing my work from my self-defense workshops to my health coaching. I'm sure that fear stopped me in countless ways in my twenties and thirties. Now I am crystal clear that I stand for the safety, empowerment, and well-being of women everywhere. So, when I read comments on my YouTube videos like . . .

- "Female self-defense guru? Ha! Go back to the kitchen and make a sandwich."

- Or, "Jen is such a fake and an asshole loser."

- Or even, "She is a man hater! A big man could kill her
  with one hard hit."

. . . I simply take a deep breath and shake it off. I refuse to succumb
to bullies.

It's one thing to blow off comments from misogynistic trolls
trapped behind their computer screens. It's another to receive
criticism from people I know and respect. But as a black belt, I'm
open to learning and improving, knowing full well I do not have
all the answers. I know that in taking a stand for a cause bigger
than myself, I will make mistakes, and I will fail. I'll experience
moments and seasons that suck and bring me all the way back to
my white belt lessons. I must always practice all belt levels because
I know life will keep testing me to make sure I know what I stand
for. In the meantime, I'll keep sharing, teaching, speaking up, and
showing up.

So what about you? What do you stand for? What motivates
you to keep working the levels, to keep showing up?

You may know exactly what you stand for. That's amazing!
You've been practicing your black belt skills all along (but don't
forget to keep practicing your white through red belt lessons so
you don't crash and burn by forgetting how to bounce back, set
boundaries, use your voice, or protect your energy). But many of
us aren't so clear about what we stand for. It's easy to get caught up
in the hustle and bustle of life and lose sight of the bigger picture.
We forget we're here for a larger purpose than just to earn a pay-
check, buy a bunch of crap, and die. It's normal to feel like there's
no more time in your already packed schedule, or that you don't
have the resources to make a difference. But as a black belt, you'll
realize you do have plenty to contribute to a cause that speaks to

you. And when you find your stance and make the effort, you'll feel stronger, more capable, and more badass than ever before.

Exercise: Finding Your Stance

In martial arts, there are physical stances we practice over and over. Front stance, back stance, and horse stance, to name a few. All of them are drilled repeatedly as a way to keep your balance and not get knocked down in a fight. In life, finding your stance is about staying upright and steadfast in the face of adversity, unfairness, or inequality.

I became serious about teaching women's self-defense after I was grabbed that night on the street. I wanted to make sure other women had the skills to protect themselves too. I was enraged when I read statistics on sexual assault and started hearing stories from women who had been in much worse situations. I thought if I could stop just one woman from being a victim of assault, all the effort would be worth it.

I now stand for women's safety, probably because some asshole decided to put his hands up my dress one night in the East Village. Sometimes we're called to fight for things because we've experienced the discomfort or injustice ourselves. Sometimes we find our stance through watching others suffer through pain and injustice, and it tugs on our heartstrings, whispering to our spirit to jump in and help. Your stance is the thing that makes your eyes twinkle when you talk about it or can get you into a heated argument when people just don't understand. It lights up your soul to even imagine how you can make a small difference in something so much larger than yourself.

Here are some writing prompts to help you find that soul-shifting thing for you. Take a moment to complete the sentences with the first thoughts that come to mind.

1. When I hear a story about _____, my blood boils.
2. When I see someone do _____, it hurts my soul to watch it.
3. When I'm watching the news and _____ happens, I scream at the TV.
4. When I see someone help _____, I just melt.
5. When I hear of people, places, or things that are suffering from _____, I want to help by _____.
6. In my community, there are people who don't have _____, and I know I can make their world just slightly better.

After completing the prompts, do you notice any themes? Is there a particular group of people you really care for? Is there a disease or condition that affects you or someone in your life? Are animals or the planet part of your stance? Write down three areas where you may find your stance.

If it's a topic that you are against, try finding your stance in the opposite. For example, if you are very concerned about the climate crisis, perhaps you can find your stance in practicing or educating others on sustainability. If you are against animal cruelty, you can find your stance in finding safe homes for animals. In my case, I get so angry when I hear stories of sexual assault and violence against women, and, therefore, I'm clear that I stand for women's safety.

Over time, pay attention to your stances. Read a book about the topic, listen to a podcast, or simply notice when it's in the headlines. Tune into your inner warrior to hear the tugging toward how you can contribute. Perhaps you'll be given messages on how you can align yourself with your stance and find your give. Once you know what you care about, the next step is to figure out how you can contribute in a positive way to making a change.

Finding Your Give

There are too many examples of so-called leaders making headlines about their greed for money and perceived power. It's sickening to watch politicians take illegal payments and kickbacks in exchange for favors, or watch board members and CEOs pay barely livable wages to employees while raking in millions every year. This is not the kind of leadership we want to emulate. We want more heart-forward leadership. Feminine leadership that is strong, powerful, and nurturing all at once. The type of leadership that inspires people to do better, be better, and give back.

Giving back is obviously good for our communities, and it's good for us too. Loneliness, stress, anxiety, and depression were at an all-time high pre-pandemic. Imagine what they're like now? A study by Cigna in 2019 reported that 61 percent of Americans feel lonely. One in six Americans take antidepressants. I'm not saying that black belt status is a cure for loneliness or depression, but what if it made some people feel incrementally better and more purposeful? What if it allowed people to step outside themselves and feel the powerful phenomenon of helper's high, a euphoria that happens when you do charitable deeds? What if people felt more at peace because they knew their actions were making a difference in someone else's life?

I remember when I was first called on to lead warm-ups during hapkido class. I was just a lowly orange belt at the time, and I was terrified of messing up because there were black belts in the class. Over the years, I built my teaching chops, and I began to realize the impact I could have on people. I wasn't just teaching students how to perfect their roundhouse kick or defend against knife attacks. I was helping them end their crappy day on a positive note. Or helping them feel stronger and more confident. Maybe they were inspired to stand up for themselves at work, ask for that promotion, or leave an unhealthy relationship because of their newfound strength. During my lowest days, I always kept my commitment and showed up to teach class, because I knew that once I got over my problems and my insecurities, got onto the mat, and focused on my students, my cup would be filled ten times over.

Contributing makes people feel good. Period. Making a difference in someone's life or for a cause gives you a sense of genuine purpose and power like nothing else. Whether you consider yourself an introvert or a loudmouth, a doer or a thinker, there's plenty of space for you to contribute in a way that makes a difference and makes you feel awesome. We often think writing checks and sending Venmo payments are the only ways to give back, but money is only one of countless resources you have to give. We also think our contribution won't be big enough to make a difference, but I'm here to remind you that the smallest act of generosity, care, and kindness can brighten someone's day or move the needle enough to make a significant impact. You never know how your small give may have ripple effects for years to come.

If you're not sure how you can contribute to the causes you stand for, consider the following examples and use them for clarity and inspiration.

- Are you an eloquent writer? Perhaps you can volunteer to write copy for a nonprofit's website, newsletter, or social media posts.

- Are you a talented artist but don't want to march in a protest because crowds are not your thing? Make signs that marchers can use.

- Are you a great party planner? Plan your next dinner party as a fundraiser for your favorite organization.

- Are you great with kids? Volunteer to mentor one or offer to teach a skill at the local school or Girl Scouts chapter.

- Has your life been affected by cancer or another disease? Organize a toy drive for your local children's hospital.

- Have you suffered from a miscarriage or a child loss? Be a resource for parents going through similar tragedies.

- Are you handy around the house? Sign up for a Habitat for Humanity build.

- Do you identify as LGBTQ+? Support teens who are struggling with their identity.

- Are you passionate about the health of this planet? Organize a beach cleanup.

- Do you feel like the elderly are not well treated in this country? Drop off flowers at the closest senior care home or volunteer to teach a skill there.

- Are you talented in the fields of STEM? Give back to kids who don't have access to that kind of education.

- Are you a sucker for animals? Volunteer at the nearest animal shelter or foster a cat or dog until it finds a home.

There are endless ways to give back and contribute to humanity. Every time you give, you are leading and practicing black belt skills. Everyone has something to give and every bit helps.

How often and how much of your time and resources you give is entirely up to you. Weekly, monthly, yearly giving? Whatever works in your schedule. Just remember how it feels when you do it. Remember that you have access to that warm, heart-forward feeling at any point, especially during your most stressful times in life. Giving back is a chance to reset and reconnect with your leader within, and don't be too humble to share about it! Let others know what you're up to on the chance you may inspire them to action as well.

Accountability: The Double-Edged Sword

As you worked the levels of this book, your badassery has blossomed and your leadership skills have grown exponentially. Through white and yellow belt, you built your resilience muscles so you no longer get stuck in victim mode. The orange belt lesson had you standing up for yourself more and more. Green belt helped you communicate more powerfully. During blue belt you plugged up energetic holes with self-care to free up more energy. Through red belt training you went within; now you trust yourself more, and because of that inner trust, you act with conviction. Wow! That's a lot of work. Don't you think that people in your life are starting to notice a change in you?

With this enhanced power and confidence comes visibility and with visibility comes more accountability. People in your circles start to look to you for guidance or help. Your words carry more weight. The power that comes from you can be used to influence people, shift perceptions, motivate, and inspire. It's an honor to be able to have that type of presence in a community. But power and leadership are like a double-edged sword. They can be used for good or not. They can be used to heal or harm. Your message and purpose will be held in regard, AND you will be held to a higher standard. That's where responsibility comes into play.

Taking responsibility for your words and actions is not for the weak. It's hard work to consistently check in with yourself and make sure your intentions, words, and actions are in alignment. When we fall out of alignment, we may get called out by others or met with skepticism or distrust. But please remember this: It's more than okay to mess up! You may say something inappropriate, use an outdated term, back someone or something you once thought worthy of your attention but may no longer be. It happens. We're human. As long as we can be open to learning from our mistakes, we can bounce back and do better. But not putting ourselves out there because we fear messing up would be a worse mistake.

I wear many hats in my career and one of them has been as a nutritionist at mental health treatment centers for teens. I speak to teenage kids who suffer with eating disorders and poor body image. In this role, I need to be completely authentic so kids trust me and open up about their issues. I need to practice empathy so I can meet them where they are at and try to help them from there. In order to consistently stay authentic, I have to make sure

I practice body positivity for myself. Not just in front of them, but throughout my life. I check myself when I speak about food and healthy eating habits. I won't trash-talk my body in front of my friends, even when it's oh so tempting to do so. I won't food shame others or myself for unhealthy choices. I do my best to make sure I walk the walk before I talk the talk. But I'm human. And I mess up in this category, a lot.

There are days when my muffin top just pisses me off or I won't post a picture of myself if my nose is accentuated by the camera angle. I feel a little guilty about that extra slice of pizza or food shame my husband for his late-night Pim's cookies addiction. I become more aware of it, and I do my best to correct the behavior before it snowballs. I meet myself with empathy and remind myself I do really love and appreciate my body. I remind myself I'm healthy and that treating myself to foods that make me happy from time to time is part of my healthy lifestyle. I can apologize to my husband for the cookie shaming. Most important, I remember I am a black belt in badassery and that means I am a constant work in progress. Falling out of alignment and straightening myself back up again and again is my work.

You can remind yourself of that too. The next time you mess up and you fall out of alignment with who you aim to be, meet yourself with empathy and remember that you too are a beautiful work in progress. This is the way of the black belt. The next time you make a promise you can't keep or act in a way that does not make you feel good about yourself, acknowledge the mistake, correct it if you can, and move on. Let's practice it with our words.

Getting into Alignment Exercise

For the next twenty-four hours, practice the following:

1. Stick to your commitments. Do what you said you will do for both yourself and others. Make no excuses, and prove to yourself that your word matters. Did you promise yourself you would squeeze in a thirty-minute workout? Make it happen. Did you promise your boss or a client you'd finish a project? Get 'er done. Did you tell your mom you'd call her back? Pick up that phone. Practice keeping your word, and the more you do, the more careful with it you will be.

2. Do not make any empty new promises. Whether the promises are to yourself, your kids, or work colleagues, only commit to actions you can absolutely deliver on.

3. If you do slip up, own it. We can't always stick to our commitments because shit occasionally happens that's out of our control. When that happens with commitments to others, have the difficult conversations to own your missteps. When it's with yourself, you can do the same. Letting yourself down sucks sometimes even more than letting someone else down. The more you do it, the less trust you have in yourself. Apologize to yourself for breaking your word and put in place a promise or commitment that you can stick to instead.

The more you practice this, the more you will see that your words and actions matter. You'll realize the impact you have on others around you as well as on yourself, your mood, and your confidence. The more you keep your word, the happier you will be with yourself, and the more confident you'll feel as you lead in your communities.

A Rising Tide

My wish is that everyone who reads this book will implement the way of the black belt in your homes, at your workplace, and on the street. Where you travel and where you live. Remember that we're all just works in progress, doing our best to make our sliver of this world a better place. By taking the lead in your community, you may receive great accolades and notoriety, and you may not. Either way, I can promise you this: the more you help lift others up around you, the greater we all become for it. "A rising tide lifts all boats" is a phrase that's been used in politics regarding financial policies. But I can't think of a better visual for the way of the black belt than that.

Fellow black belts, we are the tide. And if you're reading this book, most likely you're a woman, identify as a woman, or are an ally of women. We need to raise the tide for all of us and especially those who have been forgotten about in their sinking boats. We need to raise the tide and help pull others up with it.

When I was a young girl, I played with Barbies, I loved my Easy-Bake Oven, and I proudly wore my multicolored sequined tutu at dance recitals. As a teenager, I learned how to take care of a baby (aka, a bag of flour) in home economics class, and on Friday nights I couldn't wait to put on my short, pleated skirt and tight sweater uniform to cheer on the boys playing football. I'm not saying there was anything wrong with my upbringing, but I'm pretty certain I'm not alone in saying I wasn't learning how to fight for a better world where women aren't objectified, where women could feel safe walking the street at night, or where women can choose their own life path without the constant judgment and restrictions of others.

Times are changing, of course. Barbie launched a line of politically themed dolls and young girls are reading the Little Feminist book series. #MeToo and #TimesUp have shined some light on the assault and harassment that many women experience. But there's still more work to be done. How do we consistently keep standing up for ourselves and for other women when sometimes it can feel like a losing battle?

There are so many women I admire who have dedicated their lives to taking a stand for women in the world. Oprah Winfrey. Gloria Steinem. Ruth Bader Ginsburg. Malala Yousafzai. The list is long. And it can sometimes feel like my work and my giveback are so miniscule compared to the impact that women like these have on the world. But then I remember we're all in this together. Small contributions from many can make massive change for all. You don't have to start a nonprofit or be nominated for a Nobel Peace Prize to practice your black belt skills. Everyone has the ability to make a difference for womankind.

I struggled with writing this book for women versus keeping it gender neutral. People advised me against it. I was told I could sell more books if *The Art of Badassery* wasn't pigeon-holed as a woman's book. Everyone on my team struggled with placing a woman on the cover or not. But at some point, I put a stake in the ground and chose to go for it, **because I stand for the safety and empowerment of women.** Why WOULDN'T I write a book for women? Why would I let the opinions of others cloud my vision? We all get cloudy from time to time, and then we remind ourselves of our stance. We can thank everyone for their opinions (or not) and move on. We plant our feet firmly to the ground and become steadfast and unshakeable once again.

Whether you're a woman reading this book or not, I hope you'll share my stance on women's safety and empowerment. Isn't it about time that women can feel safe and confident in this world? We all know what we're up against and lest we forget: Women are still being denied equal pay in some organizations, women shoulder the bulk of the burden at home, and the prevalence of sexual harassment, assault, domestic abuse, and rape *is abhorrent* in our society and around the world.

In corporate America, only 8.1 percent of the Fortune 500 list companies have female CEOs as of June 2021. As of 2021, women hold only 26.9 percent of the total 535 seats of the US Congress. Women represent just 24 percent of the US Senate and 27.6 percent in the US House of Representatives. Roughly, women account for half of the population, but we are represented by only a quarter of the leadership positions in our government. Misogyny and violence against women are still very real. One in three women globally will be the victim of sexual violence according to the World Health Organization. And just to be crystal clear, the violence is at the hands of men with a deep hatred and resentment of women. We carry this burden always but never alone. We carry this burden together as women.

If the previous statistics make you uncomfortable or even angry, GOOD! They should! We need to fully embrace our anger and not be afraid of it. We can harness anger into fuel that keeps us moving toward equality and empowerment for ourselves and the next generations.

If you find you have space in your life to step into your black belt role, then you can take a stand for us all. This is where we teach girls and young women to stick up for themselves and fight back. Where we stop saying "Boys will be boys" and "It's just locker-room talk." Where we no longer tolerate misogynistic jokes or watch our bosses berate the intern. Where we call out sexist and predatory behavior in schools, sports, religious organizations, places of business, and our homes. This is where we take a stand for safety and empowerment of all women, not just the ones that live under our roofs. This is where we rise, together.

There are countless ways we can support one another. And to be clear, I'm not saying that just because you are a woman or identify as a woman that you must support every woman in your life. There are toxic women out there too: the mean, vindictive boss; the gossip queen; the woman who will sleep with your partner; and the ones in the public eye who are up to no good. I'm not asking you to support them too. We can ignore them and be a better example of how women lift one another up and not tear one another down.

There are many ways, large and small, that we can stand for women. I bet you're already helping women in your own way, but just in case you could use a little inspiration, here's a list of twenty-six ways we can make the world just a little better. Some are free and take very little effort. Others will require more effort and time. Whatever you choose is just perfect. You are now a black belt for life, and taking a stand is not a one-time exercise but an ongoing way of life. This is the way of the black belt.

26 WAYS TO TAKE A STAND FOR WOMEN

1. Buy a coffee or tea for a woman at the office who you know is going through a difficult time.

2. Help a woman carry her baby stroller down the subway, train, or bus stairs.

3. Compliment a woman for her wit, intelligence, or creativity.

4. Tell a young woman that her needs, wants, and desires are just as important as her male counterparts'.

5. Teach young women how to achieve financial independence. Share tips you've learned about the stock market or crypto currency.

6. Hire and promote women in the workplace, in your business, and in your home.

7. Mentor a girl or woman in your career or your personal life. You have gifts to share as a mentor for someone coming up without the resources you may have had.

8. Cast a vote. Vote for government officials who support women's rights and equality.

9. Purchase from women-owned brands.

10. Start a book club and choose books by women authors, or choose books that promote women's equality or share stories of women.

11. Donate your professional clothes to a charity like Dress for Success whose mission is to empower women to achieve economic independence.

12. Start a clothing drive at work to donate to a nonprofit organization.

13. Start a fundraiser for a women's organization you would like to support.

14. Educate yourself on women's issues. Even if you are not facing them personally, read about groups of oppressed women around the world and the unique challenges they are facing.

15. Use social media to share a post or an article that brings awareness to women's issues and/or supports women's equality and empowerment.

16. Start a women's group in your company or organization. Many large corporations do this already, but if your place of work doesn't have one, create one.

17. Start a women's mastermind group if you are an entrepreneur. Meet monthly and support one another in business.

18. Stop purchasing from brands that objectify women.

19. Stop consuming media that objectifies women.

20. Call out misogyny and sexism. Whether in the office or at the dinner table. Tell folks you're not here for it.

21. Listen to women who are victims of abuse, assault, and inequality. Create a safe place to allow women to share their stories.

22. Believe women's stories of abuse, assault, and inequality. Stop asking questions like, "Why does she stay in an abusive relationship?" or "Why didn't she fight back?"

23. Stand up for a woman who is being slut-shamed, body-shamed, or bullied in any way.

24. Speak kindly and listen to elderly women. They've been around the block and have wisdom to share.

25. Donate some cash money to a charity that supports the empowerment, safety, and well-being of women.
26. Be a Nancy (from my September 11 story). If you see a woman in a state of distress, help her. Keep her calm. Help her figure out the next right step.

Although we are at the end of this journey together, grasshopper, it is not over. In martial arts, achieving black belt status is not the end, it's only the beginning. On the mat, a black belt means you have mastered your basic skills and now it's time for more advanced training. In the dojo of your life, your self-development journey never ends. You will continue to be tested, and you will continue to put your skills to the test. You'll get knocked down and get back up again. You'll have negativity thrown your way, and you will use your blocks. You'll be challenged to use your roar, and you'll own it. You'll get tired, and you will recalibrate with radical self-care. You'll be tempted to get caught up in the outside noise, and then you'll connect with your inner warrior for guidance and truth. You'll fall victim to a case of the "poor me's" and then you will step outside yourself and help someone up. This is the way.

Thank you for taking this trip with me, my friend. I'm truly honored. I hope you'll come back to it time and time again to sharpen your skills, to unleash your mojo, and to live a life of utter badassery.

ACKNOWLEDGMENTS

To everyone who has supported me during this book-writing journey, I want to applaud and acknowledge you. To my husband, Lindsay, thank you for believing in me and your steadfast love that helps keep me grounded. To Mom, Dad (in spirit), Anthony, and Julia, I love you and couldn't write a book about badassery without being raised by badass parents and having fiercely loving siblings.

To all of my writing-circle friends, thanks for the motivation to consistently get my butt in the chair to write. Christa Bourg, your wordsmithing and feedback helped shape the content of this book, and I couldn't be more grateful to you. To my agent Michele Martin, and to editor Allison Janse, and the rest of the HCI team, you have been nothing short of a blessing, and I thank you for getting this book out into the world.

To all my teachers at the World Martial Arts Center in NYC, thank you for fostering a love of martial arts and a warrior spirit in me that has shaped so much of my career and my life.

To all my beautiful and supportive friends, colleagues, and allies who have contributed stories, who have been sounding boards, who have listened to me whine, and who have cheered me on, I cherish you.

REFERENCES

Chapter 3: Orange Belt

Stop Street Harassment Statistic.
Stop Street Harassment. "Study on Sexual Harassment and Assault." February 21, 2018.
https://stopstreetharassment.org/our-work/nationalstudy/2018-national-sexual-abuse-report/

WHO Statistic.
World Health Organization. "Violence Against Women." March 9, 2021.
https://www.who.int/news-room/fact-sheets/detail/violence-against-women

Chapter 5: Blue Belt

Gallup Poll Workplace Burnout.
Gallup Poll "Employee Burnout, Part I: The 5 Main Causes." July 12, 2018.
https://www.gallup.com/workplace/237059/employee-burnout-part-main-causes.aspx

Gallup Poll Household Chores.
Gallup Poll "Women Still Handle Main Household Tasks in U.S." January 29, 2020.
https://news.gallup.com/poll/283979/women-handle-main-household-tasks.aspx

Blue Cross Blue Shield Millennial Study.
Blue Cross Blue Shield "A Focus on Millennial Health Trends." April 24, 2019.
https://www.bcbs.com/the-health-of-america/reports/the-health-of-millennials

Chapter 7: Black Belt

Fortune 500 List
Fortune, "The Female CEOs on This Year's Fortune 500 Just Broke Three All-Time Records." June 2, 2021.
https://fortune.com/2021/06/02/female-ceos-fortune-500-2021-women-ceo-list-roz-brewer-walgreens-karen-lynch-cvs-thasunda-brown-duckett-tiaa/

Cigna Loneliness Study
Cigna. 2020 U.S. Report, "Loneliness and the Workplace."
https://www.cigna.com/static/www-cigna-com/docs/about-us/newsroom/studies-and-reports/combatting-loneliness/cigna-2020-loneliness-factsheet.pdf

ABOUT THE AUTHOR

Jennifer Cassetta is a nationally recognized motivational speaker and health and empowerment coach with a third-degree black belt in hapkido and a master's degree in nutrition. Over the past two decades, she has helped people feel

Photo by Michael Cinquino

strong, safe, and powerful from the streets to the boardroom. Her keynotes and trainings have helped tens of thousands of women tap into their innate power, speak up against predatory behavior, and level up their mind, body, and spiritual well-being.

From teaching Carrie Fisher self-defense on the *Today* show to being a featured weight loss expert on ABC-TV's *My Diet Is Better Than Yours,* Jenn brings a unique passion, plus practical tips for self-defense, optimal mental and physical health, and personal badassery.

Visit jennifercassetta.com or
@jenncassetta on Instagram and TikTok

For speaking engagement inquiries, visit:
jennifercassetta.com/talk-to-me